PUB WALKS
—IN—
Herefordshire

PUB WALKS
IN
Herefordshire

THIRTY CIRCULAR WALKS
AROUND HEREFORDSHIRE INNS

Eleanor Smith

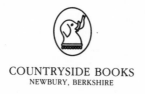

COUNTRYSIDE BOOKS
NEWBURY, BERKSHIRE

First Published 1994
© Eleanor Smith 1994

COUNTRYSIDE BOOKS
3 Catherine Road
Newbury, Berkshire

ISBN 1 85306 271 5

Designed by Mon Mohan
Cover illustration by Colin Doggett
Photographs by the author
Maps by Wendy Bernhard

Produced through MRM Associates Ltd., Reading
Typeset by Paragon Typesetters, Queensferry, Clwyd
Printed in England

To my husband Joe

Contents

Introduction   9

Walk   1   Leintwardine: The Lion Hotel (6 miles)   12

     2   Orleton: The Boot Inn (3 miles)   16

     3   Yarpole: The Bell Inn (5 miles)   19

     4   Tenbury Wells: The Fountain Inn (2½ miles)   23

     5   Leominster: The Black Swan (2½ miles)   27

     6   Bromyard: The Crown and Sceptre (4½ miles)   31

     7   Bromyard Downs: The Royal Oak (6 miles)   35

     8   Fromes Hill: The Wheatsheaf (6 miles)   38

     9   Ledbury: The Seven Stars (4 miles)   42

     10   Wellington Heath: The Farmer's Arms (6 miles)   46

     11   Much Marcle: The Slip Tavern (5 miles)   50

     12   Woolhope: The Butcher's Arms (4 miles)   54

     13   Fownhope: The Forge and Ferry (6 miles)   57

     14   near Fownhope: Gurney's Oak Inn (4½ miles)   61

     15   Hoarwithy: The New Harp Inn (4 miles)   65

     or Cottage of Content at Carey

     16   Goodrich: The Cross Keys Inn (5 miles)   69

     17   Coughton: The Crown Inn (5 miles)   73

     18   Much Birch: The Axe and Cleaver (4½ miles)   77

19   Ruckhall: The Ancient Camp (2½ or 4 miles)   81

20   Orcop: The Fountain Inn (5 or 6½ miles)   85

21   Abbey Dore: The Neville Arms (3½ or 5 miles)   89

22   Bredwardine: The Red Lion Hotel (5 miles)   94

23   Hay-on-Wye: The Old Black Lion (3 miles)   97

24   Whitney-on-Wye: The Boat Inn (2¾ miles)   101

25   Kington: The Swan Hotel (4 miles)   104

26   Pembridge: The New Inn (3½ miles)   107

27   Shobdon: The Bateman Arms (4½ miles)   111

28   Weobley: Ye Olde Salutation Inn (4 miles)   115

29   Marden: The Volunteer Inn (3 or 4 miles)   119

30   Hereford: The Castle Pool Hotel (3 miles)   123

Publisher's Note

We hope that you obtain considerable enjoyment from this book; great care has been taken in its preparation. However, changes of landlord and actual closures are sadly not uncommon. Likewise, although at the time of publication all routes followed public rights of way or well-established permitted paths, diversion orders can be made and permissions withdrawn.

We cannot accept responsibility for any inaccuracies, but we are anxious that all details covering both pubs and walks are kept up to date, and would therefore welcome information from readers which would be relevant to future editions.

Area map showing locations of the walks.

Introduction

Herefordshire, as a result of the reorganisation of local government between 1972 and 1974, is now part of the county of Hereford and Worcester. Local tradition, however, dies hard and to many inhabitants the former dividing line of the two counties is still there. For the purpose of this book, we are dealing with the old county boundary of Herefordshire, which is almost circular in shape and with a circumference of 108 miles.

The only city, the county town of Hereford, is placed firmly in the centre. It is here, in the beautiful cathedral, that the famous Mappa Mundi can be seen.

The geology of the county affords no significant mineral deposits of coal, iron or lead. Today, only limestone is quarried. In the south east, blue-grey limestone predominates in the scenic features of caves and cliffs where the river Wye wanders its way round to Symonds Yat. Almost the whole surface area of the county is covered with old red sandstone, about 4 million years old. It is this stone which breaks down into the rich clay soil and red loam so suitable for the growing of crops such as corn, hops and fruit.

One might liken the county's contours to a saucer. Its low-lying centre is surrounded by hills: the Malverns to the east, topping 1,000 ft, and the Black Mountains to the west. The Silurian edges of Shropshire to the north form an upland, rising to almost 1,000 ft near Leintwardine. To the south, Garway Hill climbs to 1,200 ft with uplands running to Great Doward.

Five major rivers flow through the county. The Arrow joins the Lugg near Leominster and flows north-south, joined by the Frome at Hampton Bishop, south of Hereford. Both rivers then flow together into the Wye, which wanders southward towards Welsh Bicknor and forms the southern boundary of the county. Ledbury has its own river, the Leadon, which flows into the Severn at Gloucester. It is not surprising that central Herefordshire is more a landscape of water-meadows than hillsides.

The county still retains its agricultural background and has no major industrial town. Light industry, however, flourishes, along with quarrying, cider mills and furniture workshops. The railway came to Herefordshire in 1853, thus making access easier for the thousands of Black Country families who travelled each year to strip the hop yards. The hop fields are still there but the oast houses nearby are now mostly converted into homes, still playing their picturesque part in the county's scenery.

Habitation has always been determined by physical features and nomadic prehistoric tribes would keep to the uplands and ridges, avoiding the undrained marshes of the lowlands. A burial chamber from around 2,000 BC, at the Department of Environment site above Dorstone, is attributed to the legendary King Arthur and known as Arthur's Stone. Other gravestones, quoits and cromlechs have been found in many parts of the county and include a long barrow within the hill fort near Eastnor.

The walks are mostly low in miles, making them suitable for both family groups and more mature persons. They are intended as a half-day outing and many include some interesting monument or building. The sketch map which accompanies each walk is designed to give a simple yet accurate idea of the route to be taken. For those who like a more detailed map, the relevant Ordnance Survey Landranger sheet is recommended.

Whether one walks 2, 5 or 10 miles, a source of refreshment is a necessary ingredient for a good excursion. Each walk is centred on a pub which offers well-cooked food and a selection of beers and ales. All are noted for their hospitality and provide a warm welcome to their customers. Opening times vary according to seasonal needs, but they are invariably open between 12 noon and 2 pm and again in the evening between 6.30 pm and 10.30 pm. Significant differences are noted in the text. All the establishments have been 'sampled' by the author and a brief description of each is provided, with any historical details. Most have a family room or garden area suitable for children. Where vegetarian meals are provided it has been noted.

It is as well to remember that car parking at pubs is at the landlord's discretion. If you are taking the walk without using the facilities of the pub, then you should leave the car elsewhere. If you are walking and then eating, it would be courteous to ask permission prior to leaving your vehicle in the pub's car park. Bear in mind, too, that, following a walk, one may be muddy or wet. It may be polite to leave dirty boots in the car along with wet weather wear.

The Country Code, which should be observed at all times, is as follows:

Enjoy the countryside and respect its life and work
Guard against all risks of fire
Fasten all gates
Keep your dogs under close control
Keep to public paths across farmland
Use gates and stiles to cross fences, hedges and walls
Leave livestock, crops and machinery alone
Take your litter home

Help to keep all water clean
Protect wildlife, plants and trees
Take special care on country roads
Make no unnecessary noise.

With this in mind, take your time, your camera and binoculars and enjoy your walks around the pubs of Herefordshire.

Eleanor Smith
spring 1994

Map Symbols

Church	♁
Buildings	▫
Walk route	→ → →
Road/lane	═══
River/canal	～～～
Bridge	)(
Track/footpath	═══ ─ ─ ─
Railway	┼┼┼┼┼┼┼┼┼
Place of interest or antiquity	⊗

Sketches shown not to scale.

1 **Leintwardine**
The Lion Hotel

The Lion Hotel, a large, comfortable, ivy-clad pub, retains the flavour of the old coaching inn of bygone days. Part of its history was uncovered when recent alterations unearthed part of the old stables, which are now incorporated in the lounge. The traveller of today would never guess that this hostelry once housed prisoners of the 1939–45 war. Its pretty garden overlooks the river Clun and the well-furnished restaurant and lounge offer a comfortable place to eat, drink and relax. Accommodation is also available.

Three cask beers, Whitbread, Flowers Original and Boddingtons, are served. Keg includes Marston's Pedigree and Flowers Best Bitter. Murphy's and Guinness are on tap. Cider is a popular drink in this area and varieties available here are Scrumpy Jack, Strongbow and GL Sweet. There is a comprehensive wine list and the house wine can be recommended. Food is home-made with a real Indian curry, prepared by mine host, as the speciality of the house. Sandwiches, rolls and jacket potatoes are good for a lighter meal, while home-made steak and kidney pie or a full 1 lb T-bone steak are for the really hungry walker. An à la carte restaurant menu is available with a good range of starters, main courses and sweets. The vegetarian should be well satisfied with the excellent vegetable moussaka or the bean casserole.

Telephone: 054 73 203.

How to get there: The Lion is situated on the A4113, the Ludlow to Knighton road. It is just by the bridge over the Clun and on the south side of the river.

Parking: There is ample parking at the pub, and some further parking available adjacent to the village green opposite.

Length of the walk: 6 miles. Map: OS Landranger 148 Presteigne and Hay-on-Wye area (inn GR 405743).

Leintwardine is the site of an old Roman settlement, close to the border with Shropshire and the place where the rivers Clun and Teme meet. Walk through the wide watermeadows then climb up through leafy tracks to the Downton Estate. Paths are well signed, stiles in good order – take your time and enjoy the sights and sounds around you.

Footpaths should be strictly adhered to and dogs kept on a lead through the Downton Estate land. This is pheasant country and gamekeepers are about.

The Walk

From the pub, cross over the A4113 and walk alongside the village green towards the fire station and fish and chip shop. Pass the Sun Inn and, just before reaching the sewage works, take a footpath sign pointing to the right. Follow the boundary of the works, then go round a separate shed on the left to where you will see a stile. Cross over this and bear diagonally right, across the field towards the river Clun. Unless you particularly wish to walk along the river then it is much easier to take a line above the trees and bushes above it.

Walk through the watermeadows for about ¼ mile and you will notice traffic on an adjacent lane. Still keeping in the fields, pass a farm on your left and, again, I would suggest that you keep fairly close to the left hand hedge. The river twists and turns here and, although there is a path alongside it, you will add a considerable distance to the walk if you follow its meanderings. Continue for about another ¾ mile in the meadows and, after crossing a stile adjacent to an iron gate, look for a solitary oak tree on a bank. Make for this. In the hedge just above it you will see a stile onto a lane. Go over this and turn left.

In about 150 yards there is a sign on the right for Standledene House. Just here are two gates with a footpath sign. Go through the right hand gate and head diagonally up the bank until meeting the

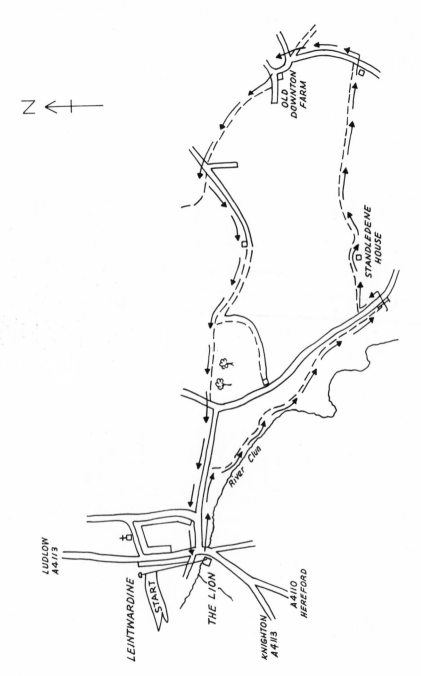

N ←

OLD DOWNTON FARM

STANDLEDENE HOUSE

River Clun

LUDLOW A4113

LEINTWARDINE

START

THE LION

KNIGHTON A4113

A4110 HEREFORD

14

hedgerow. Keep the hedge on the right, passing the house. Go over the next stile on the right, waymarked. You can now see the next two stiles ahead. Cross the paddock diagonally. Walk along the path to the gate with the double footpath sign. Head straight across the next field. There is no visible path here, but make for two trees, one of them dead. Take the old gateway round the dead tree and look right, ahead, to the next waymark sign. Bear slightly left and look for a stile in a fence. Continue on the same line to the stile on to a public road. Turn left. At the sharp right hand bend go straight ahead into the farmyard of Old Downton Farm. Turn left at the footpath sign through the buildings. Carry on this track to the last pair of gates and bear right through the white gate. You are now in pheasant cover.

There is no track here, but bear right and look for a stile in the fence. Go over the stile, a double one, and follow the line of trees, uphill, to the left. Reach a junction of estate roads and bear left (rather than double back), down an old lane. At the sharp left turn, downhill, take the gate on the right and bear left through some old quarry workings.

Follow the track down, keeping the woods closely on your left. At the lane, turn left for a few yards to the island with the sign for Leintwardine. Turn right and down the lane back to the fire station and your starting point.

2 Orleton
The Boot Inn

Built in the mid 16th century, this pub has lost none of its character over the years. It is beamed, spacious, comfortable and friendly, and a warm welcome awaits both visitor and local alike. For summer use, there is a barbecue area and ample outdoor seating in a pleasant, flower filled garden. An interesting feature is a tiny two roomed cottage, half-timbered and with a preservation order on it.

There is good food, home-made and generously served. A few of the favourites on the blackboard menu of daily specials are chicken, leek and ham pie, a mixed grill, cottage pie or a 10 oz rump steak. There is tuna and pasta bake for the vegetarian and a tasty sandwich or soup and roll for a lunchtime snack. Food is served each day during normal opening hours. The three real ales on tap are Hook Norton, Boddingtons and a guest beer. There are five ciders to choose from and a wine list includes a good house wine. The opening times are 12 noon to 3 pm and 6 pm to 11 pm (7 pm to 10.30 pm on Sunday).

Telephone: 0568 780228.

How to get there: Orleton is just east of the B4361 (Leominster – Ludlow road), approximately 7 miles from Leominster. Take the sign-posted turning opposite the Maidenhead Inn and continue through the village to the T junction. Turn left to the Boot Inn.

Parking: There is plenty of parking space at the pub.

Length of the walk: 3 miles. Map: OS Landranger 148 Presteigne and Hay-on-Wye area (inn GR 494672).

Some field walking with easy to follow paths. The lane walking is on narrow, little-used roads, cut through rock, tree lined and with a wealth of bird and plant life on either side. There is an opportunity to leave the route and visit the tree-topped Bircher Common or Woodcock Hill. A walk for all seasons and for all family groups.

The Walk

From the pub, take the footpath exit which leaves the car park in the left hand corner, alongside a lap fence. Go over the stile and in a few yards the path emerges onto a road and housing estate. Cross over and turn right. In a few yards, take the path directed by a footpath sign on your left. Cross over the wooden bridge and walk beside the brook

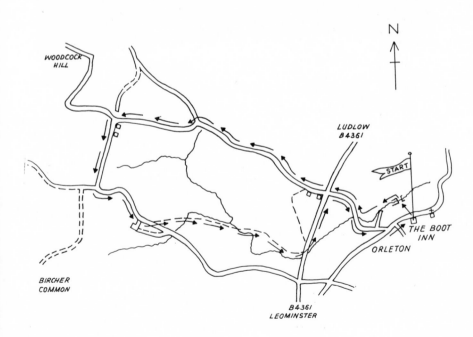

17

to a stile leading into the recreation field. Turn left and walk diagonally across the football pitch to the gap leading into the village hall car park. Turn right, into the road. On reaching the crossroads with the B4361, watch the traffic, cross over and take the lane directly opposite.

Walk up Green Lane until the first left turn. Orleton Rise Caravan Park entrance sign is on a metal gate on the right and there is a bridge over the stream. Turn left here and continue on the narrow lane, uphill. Heavy overhanging hedgerows make this a pleasant walk. At the first junction bear left. The track with the 'dead end' sign leads up to Woodcock Hill, where a diversion could be made for scenic views across the countryside.

At the next junction turn left. There is another track here up to Bircher Common. After passing a farm on your left, followed by a half-timbered house, look for a stile in the hedge on your left, about 300 yards. Cross the stile and walk diagonally, right, across the field, making for another stile, visible in the hedge. Cross the next field, following the hedgerow if planted, slightly diagonally, left, across the next and follow the path towards the road and stile adjacent to a footpath sign. You are now on the B4361 again. Take care. Turn left and in about 350 yards you are back at the Maidenhead Inn. Cross the road and follow the lane back into the village, going left at the T junction. Or you may prefer to retrace your steps through the recreation ground.

If you have time, Orleton church is worthy of a visit. It is situated just past the pub and has an early 18th century clock (not working), a 13th century oak dug-out chest with original iron straps and an impressive Norman font.

3 Yarpole
The Bell Inn

The Bell Inn, a black and white timbered building, tastefully extended, is situated in the beautiful village of Yarpole, with its charming houses, a stream and small access bridges, a church with a plaque stating that the village was recorded in the Domesday survey of 1086 and a wealth of flowers for most of the year.

Hops are the theme in this delightful pub and the decorations are suitable for this area of orchards and hop fields. A former cider house, this freehouse now serves a selection of well kept ales: Welsh Bitter, Yorkshire and Flowers real ale and the local Hobson's Choice. Bulmers cider, a variety of lagers and a good wine list, along with the usual spirits, are all available in the friendly bar. The menu varies according to season but it is safe to say that you will find the dishes cover a wide spectrum, from the humble cheese sandwich to the more exotic venison, duck or Dover sole. The inn is open, and meals are served, from 11.30 am to 2.30 pm and 6.30 pm to 11 pm. A pleasant outside seating area can be enjoyed when the weather permits and children are welcome in the eating areas.

Telephone: 0568 780359.

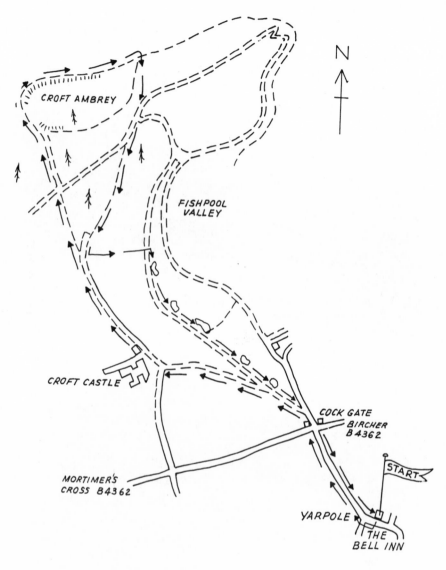

CROFT AMBREY

FISHPOOL VALLEY

CROFT CASTLE

COCK GATE
BIRCHER
B4362

MORTIMER'S
CROSS B4362

START

YARPOLE

THE
BELL INN

N

How to get there: Yarpole lies on a minor road, west of the B4361 (Leominster–Ludlow road) and south of the B4362.

Parking: At the pub or in the National Trust car park at Croft Castle, if walking from there.

Length of the walk: 5 miles (3 if leaving your car in the NT car park).
Map: OS Landranger 149 Hereford, Leominster and surrounding area
(inn GR 470650).

*An interesting walk, with views across the whole of Herefordshire from the top
of Croft Ambrey. It takes you past Croft Castle, through farmland and woods and
the beautiful Fishpool valley.*

*For a shorter walk, leave your car in the car park at Croft Castle and follow the
circular route entirely on tracks.*

The Walk

Turn right out of the car park at the Bell Inn. At the crossroads follow
the signs for Croft Castle, a National Trust property, and walk over the
cattle grid up Oak Avenue. The castle has been the home of the Croft
family since Domesday times, with a break of 170 years from 1750. It
is closed on certain days but the grounds and Croft Ambrey are open
throughout the year.

Just before reaching the entrance, turn right through a gate and
follow the signposted track to Croft Ambrey. The path continues,
uphill, with views to the left over the Black Mountains. A group of
Spanish chestnut trees will soon be reached and it is interesting to note
that these are believed to have grown from seed found in a wrecked
Spanish galleon in 1588. More of these trees can be seen if you look
down the valley beyond an avenue of limes.

You now enter a pinewood, managed by the Forestry Commission.
Still walking uphill, after passing through a gate you will be on a wide
drive. Keep straight on at the crossroads, leaving the wood and
entering an open area of bracken and trees, many of which have been
damaged by winter gales. To your left can be seen the hills of the
border region and to the right is the Whimble above New Radnor and
the Radnor Forest beside it. Pass through a gate and walk on until
reaching a stile on the right which leads to the summit of the well
preserved Iron Age hill fort of Croft Ambrey. There are many paths to
the top, so take whichever is most convenient to yourself. This fort,
along with others all over the country, was built as a defensive fort
where a whole clan could live and work. It is thought to have been
occupied for a period of 550 years, until AD 50, when the Romans
raided the site and destroyed the small wood and straw houses.

On the top, keep to the left and take the exit path. You will be
looking down on a quarry. In about 50 yards, turn right along a grass
track through open, bracken-covered land. Drop down to the forest
and walk along the perimeter fence until you reach a gate. Turn left
here and walk back along the path towards the pine woods. You will
now be retracing your steps. At the gate leading back towards the

Spanish chestnuts and the castle, turn left towards a keeper's cottage. Pass in front of this, taking care as the ground can be very slippery, and descend into Fishpool valley.

As you enter the valley by the old limekiln, you may just see the occasional kingfisher. The pools on your left are the old ponds used for keeping trout to feed the Croft family during the hundreds of years that the castle has been inhabited. Trout still rise in the pools. As you continue to follow the path you will reach a Gothic pumphouse. Just past this, the track forks. Take the left hand route which will lead you to the bottom of Oak Avenue. Retrace your steps from this point, back to the Bell Inn.

Tenbury Wells
The Fountain Inn

4

The commonlands of Herefordshire were the traditional overnight resting grounds for drovers with their herds of animals, travelling from the lush feeding grounds of the Welsh hills to the busy cities of England where the meat they produced would be marketed. This delightful black and white timbered pub is a converted farmhouse which once served the needs of these and other travellers passing from Wales into England. Cider pressing and milling went side by side here and the modern restaurant stands on the site of the old coach house.

The Fountain Inn has the 'Heartbeat Award' and is renowned for its healthy, low fat cooking, vegetarian orientated but with delicious meat dishes included in its comprehensive menu. The food is mouthwatering. Speciality ploughman's with Stilton, Brie or home-cooked ham, a sandwich selection of fresh, hand-cut chunky bread made to their own healthy recipe, and an interesting assortment of fresh salads are a few of the bar snacks. For the more leisurely meal I can recommend cold smoked trout, roast breast of chicken and bacon, succulent English beef or a salmon and broccoli pâté with a piquant sauce. Three well kept traditional ales, which include Beamish

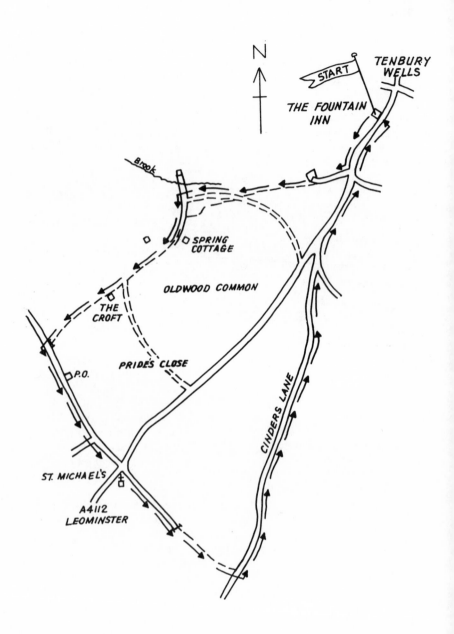

Stout and Webster's Yorkshire Bitter, are served. Dry Blackthorn is the preferred cider and many low- or non-alcohol drinks are also offered. A full wine list is available for both the bar and the restaurant.

A flower-bedecked garden and a warm welcome, which extends to children in the eating areas, make this pub a pleasant place from which to start your walk.

Telephone: 0584 810701.

How to get there: The pub is on the A4112 Leominster road, about 1½ miles south of Tenbury Wells.

Parking: There are plenty of parking spaces at the pub, and alternative parking can be found on the common, opposite the sign to Bockleton, just past the pub.

Length of the walk: 2½ miles. Map: OS Landranger 149 Hereford, Leominster and surrounding area (inn GR 590669).

A pleasant, easy walk with wide cinder tracks and criss-crossing paths, suitable for all ages and all weathers.

The route crosses Oldwood Common which, close to the boundaries of Shropshire, Herefordshire and Worcestershire, was well placed for one of the oldest flat racing tracks in the country. It attracted large crowds in its heyday. The common is now a place for recreation and wildlife. Clusters of oak and hawthorn, grasses and flowers, ponds and streams with their water life are now for us all to savour. You will also pass close to the collegiate church of St Michael, a mini cathedral set in this rural area.

The Walk

Out of the pub car park, turn right along the footpath towards Oldwood Common. At the first footpath sign on your right, leave the pavement and walk diagonally across the common, bearing to the left in front of a house. On reaching the cinder track, turn right and follow this until reaching a coppice with a brook on your right. Turn left here, passing Spring Cottage. Now swing right, past a brick and timbered house and continue along the track to a coppice of oak and hawthorn at The Croft.

Climb the stile here, at the right of the bungalow, and walk straight ahead to a stile close to an oak tree and then keep to the left hand hedge, to another stile leading onto a lane. Turn left, passing the post office. Continue walking along the lane until reaching the Leominster road.

Traffic can move quite fast along here, so beware as you cross to St Michael's church which lies opposite. The path takes you alongside the church on the left. This once provided education for the sons of poor clergymen and for wealthier families who could pay. The college closed in 1985 but the church continues with its tradition of church music by hosting many visiting choirs who consider it a privilege to sing in this treasurehouse of some of the finest craftsmanship of the period.

Walk down the lane which, quite soon, becomes just a track and then enters a field through a metal gate. Walk across this field towards Cinders Cottages with a choice of exit from the field, either in the left or right corner.

Turn left along Cinders Lane, which will bring you back to the main road again, where you turn right along the footpath to the pub and your car.

5 Leominster
The Black Swan

The town of Leominster, now peaceful enough, was once the centre of the turbulent border regions and it is certain that this inn would have participated in those troubled times. The Black Swan is, these days, a comfortable town pub. The coaching inn of old has given way to more modern conditions but retains much of its character. The beer garden has been created around the stables, behind which was the cattle market, now a stores. Clay pipes were found beneath the bar when it was altered in the 1980s. A blocked-up room, now a bathroom, was also discovered and this contained many items of clothes and, possibly, servants' toiletries, which are now displayed in the town museum. The beamed bar and lounge have the original timbers but the pub was re-fronted in Georgian times.

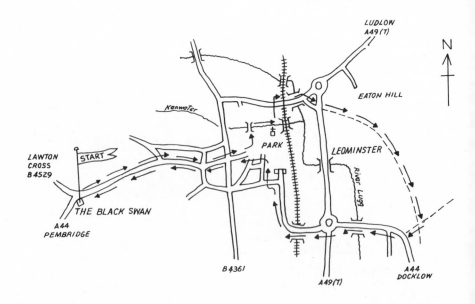

Over 30 choices are on the menu and a daily 'specials' blackboard offers the dishes of the day. A good chilli or a lasagne are popular and the Sunday lunch is quite delicious and competitively priced. Steaks, cooked to order and served with a choice of vegetables, and a home-made chicken and mushroom pie, generously served, also come well recommended. The sandwiches, served with a garnish, on good fresh bread make a tasty snack. The mouthwatering pudding menu should satisfy all comers. This is a freehouse, with a fifty-fifty split of beers, Whitbread and Bass, either of which makes for a good pint. A house wine is on tap. The opening times are 11 am to 3 pm and 6 pm to 11 pm. Accommodation is available throughout the year.

Telephone: 0568 612020.

How to get there: Leominster lies on the A44 between Worcester and Kington. The Black Swan is centrally placed in West Street.

Parking: A public car park is situated directly opposite the pub, in West Street.

Length of the walk: 2½ miles. Map: OS Landranger 149 Hereford, Leominster and surrounding area (inn GR 498595).

28

A pleasant, easy stroll over the wooded crest of Eaton Hill. The river path alongside the Kenwater is surprising in its rural atmosphere although in the centre of town. Well kept Grange Park, with black and white Grange House, adjacent to the parish church of St Peter and St Paul, is an oasis of peace.

Some road walking, a hill to climb, views over the low-lying watermeadows and the busy little town itself – variety in a short walk and one that can be enjoyed at all times of the year.

The Walk

From the pub, turn right towards the centre of the town. Continue straight over when reaching the crossroads, towards Lloyds Bank, which can be clearly seen. Keeping the bank on your left, walk along the adjacent alley. On reaching the Grange playing fields, go down the first flight of steps on your left, almost immediately. Notice the lovely black and white timbered building of Grange House on your right. Walk towards the Priory church of St Peter and St Paul and enter the churchyard. A ducking stool, now kept as a relic in the church, was the last one to be used in England. Jenny Pipes was ducked in the river Kenwater in 1809.

Make for the lower iron gate in the left hand corner. Continue down Priory Lane, a 'No Through Road', and over the Kenwater via an iron bridge. Turn right along the riverside path, where there are good views of the Priory house and church. Although you are still in the town the atmosphere is truly rural along here.

On reaching the road, the main Ludlow road, turn right. In 50 yards cross the railway track and then the bridge over the river Lugg. Immediately after crossing the river, turn right into the cattle market area (footpath sign). Cross the market towards the gate opposite (another footpath sign). Cross the Leominster bypass at this point – care needed – and immediately opposite is another footpath sign, pointing ahead along a wide track towards Eaton Hill. Follow the sign on to a wide track and make for the next gate. Go through this and, almost immediately, take the path bearing to the right. You now begin the climb up Eaton Hill and the views over Leominster and the surrounding countryside make the gentle ascent very worthwhile.

On reaching the wooded crest and an iron gate, turn right along the hedge line and over the stile. Keep right at the next stile. As the paths separate, continue keeping to the right, downhill, making for the field below. Walk along the right hand hedge of this field, with a house adjacent on the right, to the bottom hedge and a stile on to the road. You are now on the A44. Turn right, along the path and over the bridge.

There is now a choice of route. You can either take the next footpath sign in the hedge on the right and walk along the watermeadows to rejoin the path you took at the commencement of Eaton Hill, retracing your steps from there, or you can use the pavements back into town as now described.

Cross over the bypass at the roundabout and walk straight on over the railway bridge. Continue until reaching the bus station. Turn right here, Pensley Road. At the next junction, turn left and then right at the T junction. This leads back into Grange playing fields. Retrace your steps back to the inn.

Bromyard
The Crown and Sceptre

6

The Crown and Sceptre is an old inn, situated just off the centre of the town. It is hospitable, comfortable and warm in winter, the lounge having a wood-burning stove complementing the central heating. A beer garden affords views over the Bromyard Downs and is a serene spot, very attractive in summer. Children are welcome in the eating rooms and the restaurant offers a choice of good, home-made meals in addition to the bar snacks available at lunchtime. The daily blackboard 'specials' are enticing and include such appetising dishes as king prawns in garlic, pasta, mushroom and Stilton crumble or chicken tikka with rice. The home-made soup with roll or thick bread is a good warmer on a winter day, and the large filled baps are always popular. Vegetarian dishes are available.

A freehouse, the inn can serve a good pint of Banks's Bitter,

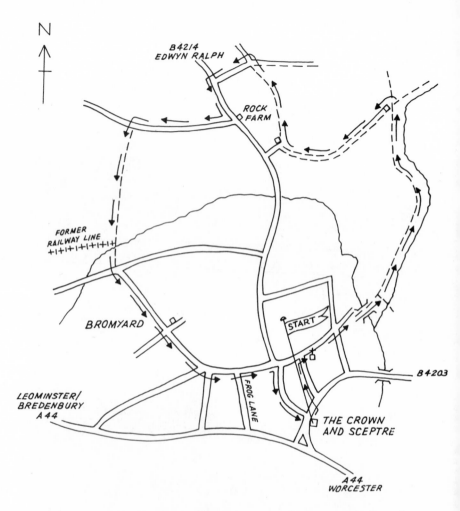

Marston's Pedigree or Hook Norton ale, tasting very good after a long walk, and the comprehensively stocked bar of spirits and wines can complement your meal. Opening times are from 11.30 am to 2.30 pm and from 6.30 pm onwards.

Telephone: 0885 482441.

How to get there: Bromyard is approximately 14 miles west of Worcester, off the A44 Leominster road. Approaching Bromyard from Worcester, turn right at town sign. The pub is on the right after about 300 yards.

Parking: There is adequate parking behind the pub.

Length of the walk: 4½ miles. Map: OS Landranger 149 Hereford, Leominster and surrounding area (inn GR 651545).

Walk alongside a stream, climb a hill, cross a disused railway line, and relish the views across the old town of Bromyard. An all-weather walk and one to give you the opportunity to admire some of the old buildings in this interesting place. A settlement since prehistoric times, close to the old salt route from Droitwich into Wales, this small market town has a wealth of history.

The Walk

Leave the Crown and Sceptre and make for the church. Walk down Church Lane, passing the Old Grammar School, now derelict, on your right. The lane soon becomes little more than a track. On reaching a crossroads, with the Micron factory on your left, continue straight on, passing a black and white house on your right. Go over the stile and keep to the right, along the track and over the bridge. Now, turn left and follow the stream.

Keep straight on inside the fence. There is quite a good path here. Go over the next stile and keep to the right. Do not cross the bridge but continue to follow the stream. Climb the next stile, left of the gate with the yellow waymark sign. Cross the next field and go over the stile. Skirting the trees adjacent to the stream, continue to the next stile. After climbing this, turn left and make for the gate near some white houses. Keep straight ahead on the track, over the cattle grid and in about 400 yards, just before a cottage and gateway on the right, there is a stile in the hedge. Climb over this and keep to the left of the field. Still keeping to the left, you will notice Rock Farm caravan park over the hedge. Go over the next stile and make for the red-brick house ahead. Turn left here, over the cattle grid and onto a rough lane. In a few hundred yards you will reach the B4214.

Turn left, downhill, and in about 300 yards there is a turning on the right marked Wicton Farm. Take this road. Continue, passing Wallcroft House on your right and, almost immediately, there is a stile in the left hand hedge. The view from here takes the eye to Bromyard Downs, crowned with trees, and the Malvern Hills beyond, brooding over the near distance. Bromyard church tower can be seen and the old part of the town surrounding it.

Continue downhill until reaching a stile in the bottom hedge. Climb the stile, noticing the ponds with a 'hide' on your right. Walk towards a wooden gate and it is here that you cross the old, now disused, Bromyard railway line.

Go through the next wooden gate and over the bridge. A hill now

33

faces you. Walk straight up it towards a split tree. Turn right nearly at the top and follow the narrow path towards a gate. Go through the gate and keep right, continuing on the level track. Bear left at the next gate and turn left into a lane with some houses on your left. This lane leads to the A44, a busy road but with a footpath. At the next road turn left and go over the crossroads. At the next junction cross over the road, into the playing fields. Go straight over the next road and down the steps which will bring you out at Lo-Cost, next to the theatre car park. It is easy to find your way back from here to the Crown and Sceptre.

7 Bromyard Downs
The Royal Oak

The Royal Oak, originally a residential property, on the edge of the downs, is an attractive, beamed pub with bow-fronted windows. It is named after the nearby large oak trees, jubilee and broad oak. A comfortable lounge bar and dining room, oak beamed and with large bay windows, overlook the valley towards Bromyard. Traditional bar food is served all day, according to season, from an opening time of 11.30 am. Steaks, gammon and trout, all served with a selection of vegetables, make a tasty meal. Ploughman's lunches and a variety of large baps with a choice of fillings are good lunchtime snacks. Real ales include John Smith's, Directors and Webster's Yorkshire Bitter. Courage Dark Mild and Beamish Stout are on draught. Local cider is a popular drink and the usual house wines are available, nicely chilled when appropriate.

Telephone: 0885 482585.

How to get there: From Worcester, take the A44 Leominster road. Just after passing the entrance to Brockhampton Estate, take the turning to the right, signed 'Stourport'. In about 1 mile you will see the Royal Oak, on the right. The pub is at a crossroads just south of the B4203 (Bromyard–Stourport road).

35

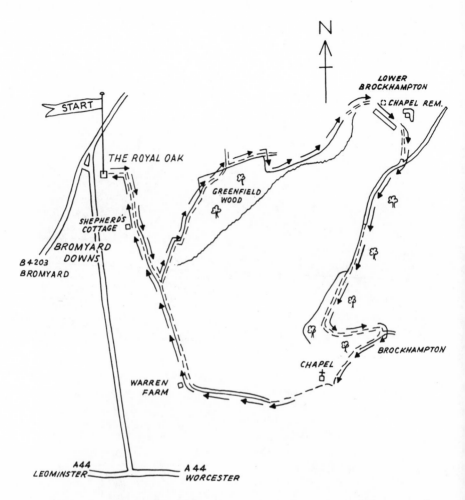

Parking: There is a large car park at the pub, and a public car park adjacent.

Length of the walk: 6 miles. Map: OS Landranger 149 Hereford, Leominster and surrounding area (inn GR 670560).

The walk starts from Bromyard Downs, a striking vantage point dominating the area around. Drovers brought their cattle here on their journey from Wales to the cities of England and it was here that the old Bromyard racecourse was a mecca for horse racing enthusiasts.

Joining the National Trust land after leaving the common, the route is well signed, passing through pasture land and woods to Lower Brockhampton, a rare delight of picturesque buildings and ponds. A steep climb, daffodil-lined in spring, takes you to the family chapel of Brockhampton Estate and you return over the downs.

This walk could well take a full day. There is so much to see that it would be a pity to hurry along in such a special place.

The Walk

Leave the Royal Oak and walk into the picnic/car park area provided by the local council. From here, take the track bearing to the left, passing behind the pub. This is part of the old racecourse. Fences and water jumps have now disappeared but the original track is still visible and is, indeed, used today by many walkers. You will, shortly, join a footpath going off to the right, uphill, making its way into the Brockhampton Estate. Turn right along the track, passing Shepherd's Cottage and then Shepherd's Pool. At a fork, turn left, almost doubling back on yourself, and follow the path around the edge of Greenfield Wood.

Bear to the right as the wood ends. It is signposted by the National Trust at regular intervals. The path ends at Lower Brockhampton, where the beautiful black and white moated farmhouse and attractive, detached, half-timbered 15th century gatehouse stand. The gatehouse is a rare example of this type of structure. Do not miss the remains of a 12th century chapel. Graceful swans enhance this lovely scene, which is very popular with local artists.

The walk back to the pub goes uphill, using the main entrance road to the property, full of daffodils in the spring. On reaching the top of the hill, on the right, surrounded by trees, you will see the family chapel. Take the track just opposite the estate yard and walk towards Warren Farm. Cross one more field and you will rejoin the track leading to Shepherd's Cottage and so back over the downs to the Royal Oak.

8 Fromes Hill
The Wheatsheaf

The Wheatsheaf, just by the summit of Fromes Hill, has much to commend it. A modernised coaching inn, it provides for all ages of customers and even has a very safe children's playground with bouncy castle and climbing frames. The surrounding 8 acres of orchards are some of Bulmers' trees for use in its cider making. A beautiful sight when in full bloom.

Not only does this pub sell beer but it also makes it, and very good it is too. Brewed twice a week, it is popular with locals and travellers alike. Christened 'Buckswood Dingle' after a local race horse, it is also used in the recipe for the pub's home-made sausages. Other brews on sale are traditional Bass and Worthington, along with Stones Best Bitter. Ciders include Bulmers Scrumpy and Red Rock Ultra Special. A wide range of whiskies takes pride of place in the bar and comfort is assured in the lounge with its open fire in winter and many chairs and couches. The traditional bar food is supplemented with good 'Round the World dishes' which include Indian and Chinese meals. A chargrill supplies lamb cutlets, double pork escalopes, sirloin and fillet steaks and the home-made Buckswood sausages. Seafood chowder comes well recommended, as do barbecued spare ribs.

For simpler fare, the home-made soup of the day is truly a speciality and sandwiches with a variety of fillings are on offer.
Telephone: 0531 640888.

How to get there: The Wheatsheaf lies on the A4103 Worcester–Hereford Road, approximately 13 miles from Worcester.

Parking: There is plenty of space at the pub.

Length of the walk: 6 miles. Map: OS Landranger 149 Hereford, Leominster and surrounding area (inn GR 681465).

The walk passes through a variety of the interesting areas of this part of the county. Relatively close to the border with Worcestershire, it is, however, very typical of Herefordshire with its black and white buildings, low-lying watermeadows and profusion of blossom in the springtime. You will walk alongside a most interesting site of ancient buildings, Old Cheyney House with its chapel and walled garden and, later, Castle Frome church with its splendid font. There is a steep climb at the end of the walk up Fromes Hill, but as this is by way of fields rather than road its gradients are considerably less. The walking is open and mostly on well worn paths or tracks (sometimes muddy) and along narrow country lanes with very little traffic.

The Walk
Leaving the inn, cross the busy A4103 and turn left onto the pavement. Pass a turning on the right and continue along the main road until nearly reaching a small, almost derelict Congregational chapel. At the side of the chapel is a footpath, rather overgrown in spring and summer. Walk along the path to a stile and go over that into the field. Cross this small field and make for the next stile. Climb this one and make for the next. Go over that and now make for the stile in the middle of the next hedge. The views from here are quite lovely as you look across the valley towards Hereford.

Now continue, downhill, towards a gap. Note the good footpath left by the farmer. Turn right and keep inside the right hand hedge, go over the stile and keep to the right, up a steep bank, then bear left and follow the path to the next stile, close to an electric pylon. Now go into the wood, keeping to the left. Walk through the woodland for a short distance. When reaching open ground again (note the superb trees), keep left along the hedge. Still keeping near to the left hand hedge, you will probably be able to make out evidence of an old green lane now, sadly, overgrown.

Make for the gate but do not go through it. Keep, instead, to the now walkable green lane, with a wire fence on your left. Walking downhill, notice the ancient buildings, on your right, of Old Cheyney

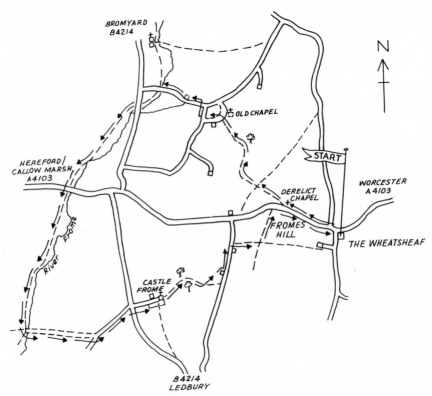

House. This mansion and farm have now been left to decay. The property was, obviously, very imposing when in its heyday and, although derelict now, has a certain beauty in the ivy-clad ruins of a former glory. The nearby pond would, probably, have supplied the estate with fish and, surrounded by bullrushes, still makes a pleasant sight. The chapel building is particularly striking and reasonably preserved. The walled garden beyond would have been the pride and joy of some head gardener of the early part of the century. Continue, keeping to the left hand wire fence, and make for the lane. Go through the gate and turn right. At the T junction turn left. After a short distance you will pass over an old bridge. The buildings and cottage could have been the mill attached to the main house.

Continue along the lane, ignoring the footpath sign on your left, to the T junction. This road is rather more busy than the lane, but in about 50 yards there is a footpath sign on the right, leading into the fields. Take this, passing through a metal gate, and turn to the left to follow the river Frome. Notice the hop field on your right. Go through the gap in the hedge, keeping quite close to the river, eventually reaching a gate leading on to the main Worcester–Hereford road – watch the traffic.

Cross the road to the waymark sign opposite and go over the stile. The footpath actually goes through the middle of the field, but it is probably just as easy to follow the river round the edge. Make for the gap and a wide track. At the end of this field, turn left over the bridge on to a track. After about ¼ mile, slightly uphill, there is a T junction. Turn left and ignore the footpath sign opposite. Continue up the lane to the Bromyard–Ledbury road.

Cross over and make for the church of Castle Frome. Pause a while and take a look at this interesting old building, situated so comfortably beneath Fromes Hill, where once the castle dominated the area. A few stones are all that remain of this today, on the high ground to the east of the church. A particularly beautiful font c.1170 has a Scandinavian influence in the decoration. Go through the churchyard to the wooden gate and pass through onto a pathway.

On reaching a stile, climb into the field and continue to walk straight ahead. In a little while bear left towards the wood on your left. You are now passing between two areas of woodland. The path goes up quite steeply. You are climbing Fromes Hill and, when nearly at the top, leave the wood and make for the house at the summit. Go over the stile into the garden. Another in the right hand hedge is visible. Cross over this into the lane and turn left.

Pass the Old Rectory and Oast House. Just past a stone cottage on your right the footpath is signposted over the stile into the field. The path goes through the centre of the field, but, if planted, it may be as well to keep to the left round the edge until reaching another stile. Go over this, and again the path goes straight ahead. You may prefer to go to the right, keeping to the side of the field, and then follow the hedge round to the gap leading on to the main A4103 again.

Turn right and cross the road on to the footpath, passing the Congregational church at the point where you began the walk, and so back to the pub.

9 Ledbury
The Seven Stars

The Seven Stars inn, built in the late 16th century, is situated in the centre of this town of timbered buildings, and overlooked the open cattle market until 1887. The old Market Hall, taking pride of place in the centre of this interesting town, leads one on to discover the Folk Museum and old Grammar School in Church Lane, and perhaps to take a peep at the medieval wall paintings in the council offices. Literary connections include John Masefield, who was born here, and Elizabeth Barrett Browning, who spent much of her childhood here.

The pub has a comfortable lounge which contains many examples of bygone country life, with implements used in the agricultural scene of the community decades ago. The dining room leads, through a short passage, to the beer garden. Unlike many outside eating areas with their lawns and children's playground, this has an old-fashioned air about it with arbours of flowers and an old pump. The food on offer – always important to the hungry walker – consists of a good choice of starters, main course and sweet. Use of the local brew in the 'scrumpy chicken dish' must be a winner. Freshly made sandwiches with crusty bread or a jacket potato with a savoury filling make a good alternative to a full meal. Marston's Pedigree, Castle Eden and Scorpio, all hand-pulled, cask-conditioned beers, are the traditional ales available. The inn can accommodate up to six guests in twin or double rooms.

Telephone: 0531 632824.

How to get there: The A438 Tewkesbury–Hereford road and the A449 Great Malvern–Ross-on-Wye road pass through Ledbury. The Seven Stars is located a few yards from the Market Hall in the High Street.

Parking: The pub does not have a car park. Public car parks are available in Bye Street, almost opposite the Seven Stars.

Length of the walk: 4 miles. Map: OS Landranger 149 Hereford, Leominster and surrounding area (inn GR 713378).

A walk with plenty of interest, well signposted with good paths, through woodland and open country, and with views across to the Malvern Hills. You will pass Eastnor Castle, designed to look like a medieval fortress, which dates from 1812. Check opening times before leaving Ledbury if you want to visit it.

This route is suitable for most family groups, having no steep climbs and little road walking.

The Walk

From the Seven Stars, walk left up the High Street, passing the Market Hall, towards the traffic lights at the top cross. Turn left. Walk as far as the police station and cross the road, where you will see the 'Walker' sign for Eastnor.

Take this footpath, go through the gate and take the left hand fork at the Y junction. The track is well defined, being in a hollow. However, it is advisable to keep slightly to the right of the hollow in order to avoid a steep bank when reaching the road. In about

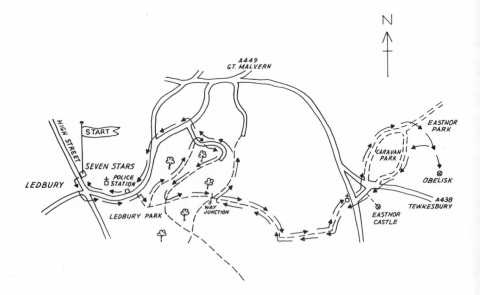

150 yards you will cross it again (it has done a U turn). The path is much used. In about 120 yards, pass through a gate on your right and emerge from the wood. Bear left along the edge of the field for about 200 yards where there is a stile at a five-way junction. This area is the site of the old Ledbury golf course.

Walk along the left hand side of the field to a gate and stile in a corner. Go through this and two similar gates and the track now climbs over a limestone ridge, typical of the western side of the Malvern Hills. There are good views across to Eastnor here. Continue on until reaching the church. Leaving the church, turn right, past the front, along the road until reaching the village green. Turn left past the primary school and some thatched cottages, including the post office. To your right is the entrance to Eastnor Castle. A memorable and romantic place, it is a major example of the Norman and Gothic revival in architecture of that time. It is open to the public on Sundays from May until October and at other times through July and August. You may well wish to divert here. Do check times of opening before leaving Ledbury.

The sloping parkland facing you is the deer park, where you may be lucky enough to see some of these shy creatures.

Cross over the A438, go through the gate opposite signed Eastnor Park and, after passing the cattle grid, in about ¾ mile you will come to Park Lodge. Turn right, going down and across the valley. In about ¾ mile is the obelisk, a memorial to members of the Somers family.

John Somers, the first Earl Somers, built Eastnor Castle. Turn back at the obelisk and follow a track along the eastern (higher) side of the caravan park. Cross the main road and follow the outward route to the five-way intersection. Turn right and through an iron gate. Walk about 140 yards along a farm track parallel with the woods (Conygree Wood). Look for a gap in the earth bank on the right and go through it. Walk for about 100 yards along a metalled track and duck under the horizontal pole. Walk down the lane to the Worcester Road, turn left and so back into Ledbury.

10 Wellington Heath
The Farmer's Arms

Wellington Heath has been a prizewinner in the Best Kept Village competition. It is a long, straggling village with an abundance of flowering shrubs and trees, well kept gardens and interesting houses. Despite its closeness to Ledbury it has a rural atmosphere, surrounded by open countryside with orchards and farms.

The Farmer's Arms was a farmhouse in Tudor times. It has been modernised but retains some of its character in the large lounge bar, which was originally the living room of the old house. A cider press in the garden is a 'left over' from the days when cider was brewed here. It would seem that, according to local tradition, cider was drunk in the farmhouse, surrounded by chickens and other farmyard animals. A far cry from the comfort of today. The bar is spacious and comfortable and leads into a well lit restaurant. Garden tables and chairs are conveniently placed, giving a delightful view over the village and orchards below.

An appetising selection of meals is offered from 12 noon to 3 pm and in the evening from 7 pm to 11 pm. Local oak-smoked salmon served on a tossed leaf salad or a delicious home-made soup are samples of the starters. Home-made chicken and mushroom or steak and kidney pie may tempt the traditionalist, while a mixed grill should provide even the most hungry of walkers with an adequate meal. Salads and ploughman's make for lighter snacks, all of which are served by the inn's friendly staff. A good pint to accompany your meal is provided with John Smith's or Ruddles ale or Directors bitter. A selection of wines, local cider and the usual spirits offer a choice to complement your meal.

Telephone: 0531 632010.

How to get there: Wellington Heath lies about 4 miles north of Ledbury and is signposted from the B4214 Bromyard road. In the village, a sign in Church Lane directs you to the Farmer's Arms.

Parking: There is parking at the pub.

Length of the walk: 6 miles. Map: OS Landranger 149 Hereford, Leominster and surrounding area (inn GR 713402).

The terrain on this relatively long circuit is very mixed, with low-lying field walking, woodland paths, a few slight hills and some road walking on narrow but little-used lanes. The route passes orchards and farms and includes Frith Wood, a landmark south east of Wellington Heath. Managed by the Forestry Commission, this woodland helps to protect the village from easterly winds. A halfway stop could be made in Ledbury by making a detour into the town before entering the woods for the return walk. It is interesting to know that, at one point on the route, you are crossing the main line railway from Worcester to Hereford by walking over the tunnel.

The Walk

From the Farmer's Arms, turn left and cross the road. The footpath sign on the right is the start of the walk. A wide track leads to a stile. After crossing this, walk across the middle of the field (there is a path visible) towards a stile in the left hand corner. Go over this and along a fenced path until reaching a wooden bridge. It can be muddy here in winter. Go over the bridge and stile, waymarked 'LR19', and continue on the fenced path, uphill, adjacent to an apple orchard. On reaching a gate and arrow sign, walk straight on, uphill, towards Frith Wood at the top.

Climb the stile at the top of the hill and turn left. This path can also be rather muddy at times and is used by horses. There is a wealth of wild flowers here in the spring, and many varieties of summer flowers, including foxgloves. The path continues alongside the wood. Views to the south west are of Wales and the Black Mountains. The path ends

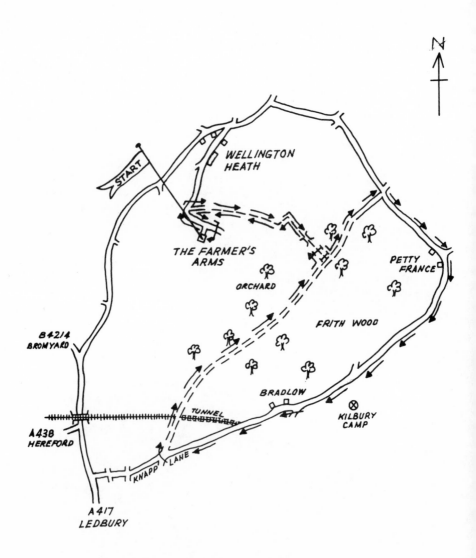

as it joins the forestry track into the woods.

Turn left here and walk along the wide track to a lane. Turn right. The lane is quite narrow and not used very much, so pleasant walking can be maintained. Pass several cottages through the village of Petty France. On reaching the T junction, turn right, signed 'Ledbury 1½ miles'. Continue walking along this lane, passing an old farmhouse with oast houses on your right. At the next fork, bear right and walk downhill until reaching the next junction. You can, at this point, cross the road and walk through the woods, keeping the lane on your right, or walk down the lane until reaching the 30 speed limit sign.

This is where you can walk down into Ledbury, if you wish to break your journey.

Immediately past the sign, on your right, is a footpath and a wide track. Walk down this track. You are now back at the perimeter of Frith Wood and it is here that you pass over the top of the railway tunnel. The footpath is easily followed along here and well marked. On reaching the large farmhouse and orchards on your left, over-looking the village of Wellington Heath, you will encounter the stile that you originally climbed to join this same path. Recross the stile and walk downhill, retracing your steps over the wooden bridge and stile and back to the lane opposite the Farmer's Arms.

Much Marcle
The Slip Tavern

Why the Slip Tavern? A very astonishing event occurred connected with Marclay Hill, as it was once known. According to a rare early 19th century book by a local historian, it was recorded that, in 1575, following a great bellowing noise, the earth began to open and a hill with a rock beneath it lifted itself up and began to travel, taking trees and sheep with it. It overthrew a chapel and thrust before it highways and hedges. This continued from the Saturday evening until the Monday noon and then stopped. There was no recorded loss of life. The chapel bell was dug up in the early 19th century. This supposed phenomenon, most probably a landslip, was given the local name of 'The Wonder'.

Now we have explained the name, we must congratulate mine host on the excellence of his garden. Flowers everywhere, hanging baskets, tubs and lawns and all in such condition that it is not surprising that it is award winning. Standing among the Weston's cider orchards, the delights of the spring blossom can only be surpassed by the rich fruit of autumn. The pub boasts a good play area for children and has plenty of outside comfortable seating for the summer days. There is a pleasant, friendly atmosphere and meals are available in dining room, bar and lounge. The menu is varied with a good value 'daily special' of which a favourite is home-cooked beef in brown ale. Beers served in this freehouse include Flowers Original and Hook Norton. Cider drinkers should be happy with Weston's and Stowford Presskeg, both local brews.

Telephone: 053 184 246.

How to get there: Much Marcle is on the A449 Ledbury to Ross-on-Wye road. Approaching from Ledbury and on reaching the village and a crossroads with Westons Garage and the PO Stores on the right hand side, turn right. Take the next right turn and you will see the Slip on the left.

Parking: There is car parking at the pub.

Length of the walk: 5 miles. Map: OS Landranger 149 Hereford, Leominster and surrounding area (inn GR 652333).

A pleasant walk around the village of Much Marcle, with an opportunity to visit Hellens House, a 15th century mansion, formerly the seat of the Wallwyn family. Open fields and one short climb bringing views across the valley to the Malvern Hills beyond. Apple blossom in the springtime and cider apples in the autumn. A typical Herefordshire scene.

The Walk

From the Slip Tavern, turn right and walk to the T junction. Notice the Jubilee tree in the centre of the road here. Turn left and continue to the crossroads. Turn right and, at the 30 speed restriction sign, turn left, between two white cottages, up a wide drive (no footpath sign). Passing some houses on your left, walk straight ahead through an iron gate. Turn right onto a wide track. As the track bends to the right, keep left along a path to a stile and metal gate. Walk diagonally across the next field, making for the right hand corner and stile. Now keep to the right hand hedge. As the hedge ends, there is a post with several waymark signs. Turn sharp right and walk parallel with the path you have just come along but on the other side of the hedge. You will now see Marcle radio mast on your right on the top of Marcle Ridge. Follow the track straight on. The tree-topped dome of May Hill can be seen to your left.

As you bend to the right you will notice the lovely old house of Hellens, a good example of a red-brick house of its time. Some parts probably date from the 15th century. It is open on Wednesdays,

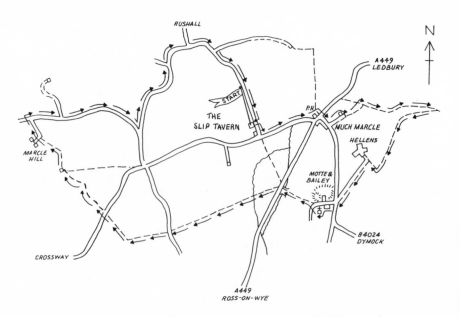

Saturdays and Sundays from Easter until the end of September.

Leaving the house on your right, turn left down the drive of the house to the road. Cross over and take the lane immediately opposite. This leads to Marcle church, which dates from the 13th and 14th centuries. The ancient yew tree just outside the main door of the church is reputedly 1,000 years old. Before following the route, it is interesting to take a look at the motte and bailey earthwork known as Mortimer's Castle. Topped with trees now, it is 21 ft in height and 170 ft in diameter. It stands just within the large iron gates immediately ahead as you approach the church.

Our walk now follows the front of the railings of the church to the gate at the end. Go through this and walk round the church path to a wooden gate on your left into a field beyond. Now go over the stile opposite into the pasture ahead. Make for the right hand corner. There is a rather strange metal gate, followed by a bridge and then a wooden gate on to a lane. Straight ahead are two footpath signs. After crossing the road, take the sign pointing diagonally left across the field.

Should you wish to curtail your walk you can now take the right hand sign and make your way back to the Slip from here. The path is clearly visible even when the field is cropped.

To continue the main walk, continue straight on across the field and walk uphill, keeping the hedge on your left. As you reach the top, take time to look across to the Malvern Hills, high on the sky line, and the village of Much Marcle nestling in the valley below. Cross over the lane and follow the footpath sign over the stile almost opposite. Cross the next field diagonally (good path visible), to a stile into a lane.

Cross over the lane and take the track opposite. This was an old hay road. Continue on the track until reaching a grey stone cottage on your left. Go over the stile in the right hand hedge, facing you. Turn left in the next field and keep along the left hand hedge. You are now quite close to the Marcle mast. Go over the next stile and turn right along the hedge. In the right hand corner is another stile. Cross this and turn right along the hedge. In the right hand corner is another stile. Make for this and turn right along the track to a lane. Turn right. Keep on the lane to the next junction and turn left. Continue on this lane bearing right past a sign for Rushall and take the road signed 'Marcle'. Make your way down this quiet lane back to the inn.

12 Woolhope
The Butcher's Arms

The name, Woolhope, is thought to derive from Wulviva. In the early 11th century, Wulviva, sister of the famous Lady Godiva of Banbury, gave the Manor of Woolhope to Hereford Cathedral.

The Butcher's Arms is a country inn originating from the 14th century. Black and white and half timbered, with low beams in the bars, it is a friendly, lively pub, with log fires in winter. The local industry of cider making is represented by the hanging bunches of hops making a traditional decoration in the lounge. There is a good patio garden beside the stream, for summer use. Accommodation is also available. A small non-smoking restaurant serves home-cooked dinners on Friday and Saturday evenings. Bar food is available at both lunchtime and in the evening and includes many unusual and interesting dishes as well as the local Herefordshire steaks. A typical menu might offer mushroom, butterbean and basil stew (absolutely delicious), rabbit and bacon pie, and lamb and cranberry casserole, to mention just a few.

A welcome pint of Hook Norton Best, Old Hooky, Marston's Pedigree or a guest beer on handpump makes a good drink after a walk, as does the local brew of Weston's cider, which is a firm favourite.

Telephone: 0432 860281.

How to get there: Woolhope is 8 miles from each of the market towns of Hereford, Ross and Ledbury. It can be reached from the A438 (Hereford–Ledbury road) through Putley or from the B4224 (Hereford–Ross road).

Parking: There is parking at the pub.

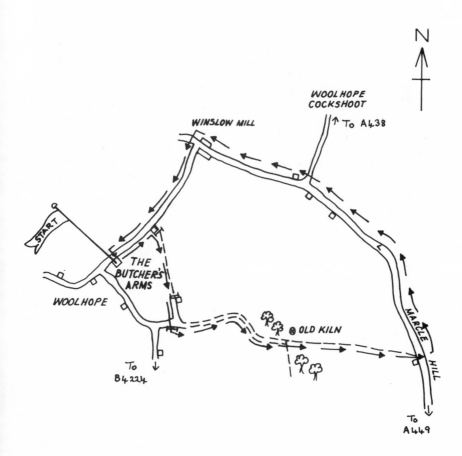

Length of the walk: 4 miles. Map: OS Landranger 149 Hereford, Leominster and surrounding area (inn GR 618362).

Woolhope is an attractive small village in an idyllic rural situation, surrounded by meadows and wooded hills. There is a field, at the beginning of the walk, one or two stiles and an interesting old limekiln beside what was obviously a well worn trail until early this century. A steep climb up on to Marcle Ridge is followed by a downhill stretch along a narrow lane to Winslow Mill. The lanes on the walk are quiet except at the peak holiday season.

The Walk

Leaving the Butcher's Arms, turn right along the lane. In about ¼ mile, close to a timbered house, there is a footpath sign on your right. Turn into this path, which goes through the drive of the house and between the property and the garage. There is a gate here. Go through this and immediately turn right along the hedge. It can be muddy here if the ploughing is close to the edge of the field. Cross the stile next to the house at the end of the field, onto a wide track. Turn left. Continue on this track, uphill, skirting the woods on the left until the path goes through a metal gate into a field. The old kiln is on your left.

Continue straight on now to the spinney ahead, where there is a stile. Go over this into the wood and make for the next stile. The field ahead is downhill. Keep to the left and then go into the next field, where you rejoin the wide track. It is uphill now, until reaching the narrow metalled lane. Turn left and walk downhill for about 1½ miles towards Winslow Mill. There are clusters of houses here and a sign-post. Bear left and continue along the lane back to the Butcher's Arms.

13 Fownhope
The Forge and Ferry

The name of this pub is self evident, coming from the joint ownership of both the ferry and the forge by one man. Much history is associated with this pub, which was originally named the Highland. The river Wye, only a few hundred yards from the pub, floods the surrounding meadows. This pub was never flooded and so became known as the 'Highland'. The present forge, now making iron gates and other items necessary in a rural community such as this, is at the top of the lane, adjacent to the B4224, but relics of the old one can be seen in the furniture of the pub. Four tables, now in the bar, were made from the original bellows, and photographs of the forge, when it was working, are to be seen, along with an original man-trap. The pub is involved with the annual 100 mile raft race which takes place along the river Wye at the end of May. Rafts are prepared here and the excitement rises as the start date approaches and the car park is alive with young men anxiously preparing their rafts to the high degree of perfection required.

The dining rooms at the inn are attractive and the lounge bar comfortable and friendly. There is both a bar and dining room menu. I tried 'Watta Roll' and it certainly was. Filled with salad, ham and

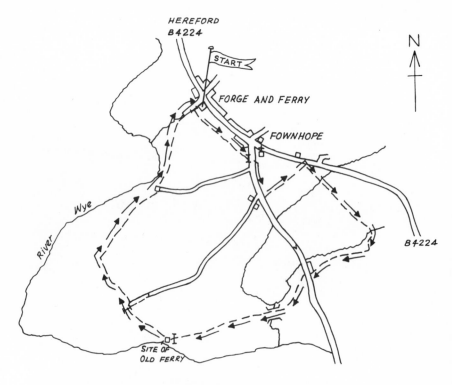

START

FORGE AND FERRY

FOWNHOPE

N

Wye

River

B4224

SITE OF
OLD FERRY

BALLINGHAM

cheese or turkey and a side order of chips this is a real filler. Soup of the day, steak sandwich and a three course Sunday lunch are also good value for money. The restaurant menu is varied and the starters include garlic mushrooms and turkey niblets stuffed with cheese. Ferryman's fish pie or venison in red wine may tempt the palate and grilled lamb chops with mint jelly or a choice of steaks are good options. Vegetarian meals are available and include macaroni and leek bake or vegetable moussaka. A children's menu provides the youngsters' favourites. To quench your thirst there is well kept real ale such as Bass or Wye Valley Hereford Supreme.

Telephone: 0432 860391.

How to get there: Fownhope is on the B4224 Hereford–Ross road. As you approach the village from Hereford, close to the general stores is a lane on the right. The pub is a few yards down this lane.

Parking: There is adequate parking at the pub.

Length of the walk: 6 miles. Map: OS Landranger 149 Hereford, Leominster and surrounding area (inn GR 578345).

Fownhope, adjacent to the river Wye, is a favourite beauty spot. This walk takes you along a scenic route with a few hills and a short distance along the riverbank. A variety of scenery, wildlife, both on the river and in the meadows, and an abundance of wild flowers make this a very pleasant halfday outing.

It is interesting to see the site of the Mansel Ferry, which crossed the river to Ballingham. The slipway is still in evidence as are the steps on the opposite bank. We can only assume that it was a foot ferry as there seems to be no evidence of any track wide enough for carts. It would have ceased to function in the 1920s, as did the one at Fownhope.

The Walk

Leaving the pub, go through the gate almost opposite the front entrance, the right hand one of two. On entering the field, keep left under the hedge, following the footpath. Go over the stile and, still keeping to the left, enter the football field. At the track, turn left and go through the gate, which brings you out opposite the church. Turn right.

Now on a lane, start to climb, steeply but gradually, until reaching Tump Farm. Opposite the entrance to the farm is a flight of steps and a stile. Go up and over. Keep to the left in the field. There is a magnificent view from here, across the village and over the river Wye. Go over the next stile and, keeping to the left, reach another stile. In this field, facing you, is a wall. Make towards the right of this and, just before reaching it, turn right along the line of trees. There is a gap in the next hedge and a bridge over a large ditch with two stiles (yellow arrows).

Continue, uphill, keeping to the right hand hedge, towards a gap into the next field. Still keeping to the right hand hedge and now climbing quite steeply, make for the stile ahead. Go straight across the next field. This could be cropped, but the path should be visible through the centre of the field. When you reach a stile (yellow arrow), pause to enjoy the view across to the dominating feature of Hay Bluff.

Now go downhill, keeping to the right over the brow of an embankment. In the right hedge at the bottom of the field is a stile (yellow arrow). Climb this and, almost immediately, go over a fence on your left. Keep to the right hedge here and, on reaching a wide track, turn right towards two gates. Take the right hand one, go through the next gap, then leave the track and make for an iron gate to your left, in the fence. Keep to the right after passing through this gate, and climb a wooden fence into a farmyard. At the steps of an old granary barn, turn right and go through the next two gates into a lane. Cross straight

59

over, climb the gate, a footpath sign here, and go straight ahead across this lovely meadow. You are making for a stile in the right hand corner of the field (yellow arrow). Ballingham now comes into view on the opposite side of the river. Cross this stile and walk diagonally right towards a bridge over a stream.

Turn right along the river bank to the next stile. Continue to follow the river, crossing stiles, until reaching the site of the old ferry and the ferryman's cottage, which is now used as a holiday home, and enjoyed without the services often considered as necessities in this day and age. Go through the gate into the cottage garden and then over a stile.

Now walk diagonally right, across the next field, and look for two stiles in the corner of the right hand hedge. Go over the stiles, cross the wide track and keep to the right under a steep bank. Still keeping to the right, make for a metal gate in the right hand hedge. Now walk up the track and, as it dies out, keep to the left of oak trees and a barn on your right. After the barn, go through the left hand gate of the next two gates and keep straight ahead to the next iron gate. Make diagonally across the field towards the trees. Go over the metal gate. Bear right slightly and then make for the left hand hedge towards the river. There is a steep drop here, which can be muddy at times.

Turn right along the river, noticing the old pump at the cottage. Go over the next stile and into the watermeadows. A fisherman's shed, on stilts, is alongside the path. Continue along the footpath on the river bank until reaching a bridge over the ditch. Go into the next field, which you cross diagonally to the right, over another bridge and then a stile. This will bring you into the lane leading to the Forge and Ferry pub.

14 near Fownhope
Gurney's Oak Inn

Gurney's Oak Inn owes its name to the original owner, when the pub was a coaching inn. The oak tree still stands behind the pub, just up the lane to the side. It is a pleasing red-brick hostelry with fine views from the garden across to Marcle Ridge. Situated on the once main route from Gloucester to Hereford, it is easy to see that it was an important place to the many travellers frequenting the road between the two cities. The pub has a comfortable lounge bar and it is now used by many groups of walkers and runners enjoying this area of particular natural beauty. A friendly welcome awaits the hungry and thirsty. Children are welcome in the eating areas, and the garden is well provided with seating.

The bar menu offers traditional meals, which include steak and kidney pie, plaice, scampi and a chicken dish of the day. Well filled omelettes of your choice are a popular lunchtime meal, and there are salads and ploughman's lunches, as well as a variety of sandwiches and a selection of sweets. A good pint of draught Hereford Bitter or Webster's Yorkshire can be enjoyed. Lagers include Foster's, Carlsberg and Red Stripe. For the cider drinker there are Bulmers Original Draught and Scrumpy Jack.

Telephone: 0989 86289.

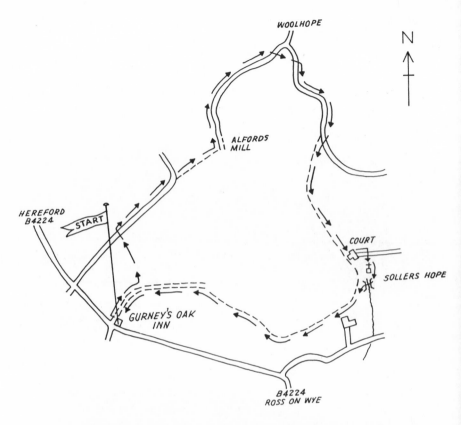

How to get there: Gurney's Oak lies on the B4224 Hereford–Ross road, approximately 2 miles south of Fownhope.

Parking: There is a large car park at the pub.

Length of the walk: 4½ miles. Map: OS Landranger 149 Hereford, Leominster and surrounding area (inn GR 605330).

Marcle Ridge towers over the lower-lying pastures of this part of the county. Truly rural, with farms dating back for hundreds of years, it has the well kept look of a caring farming community. I walked this route on a beautiful evening in May and it is difficult to find the words to describe the lush meadows, fruit trees in blossom, the variety of greens in the woodland and the hedgerows white and pink with many in full bloom. The traditional farmhouses and buildings blend perfectly with this well ordered part of Herefordshire.

The walk also passes a typical Tudor farmhouse, the home of the Whittington family for many years. It is here, we are told, that Dick Whittington was born. Other places may stake their claim to this honour but local tradition will soon counter these. It is certainly true that the Whittington family lived here in the 16th century and, while the story will have it that Dick Whittington was a poor country boy, he was, in fact, already a well-heeled gentleman who, when he reached London, became a merchant of some substance. But who are we to dispel a fairy tale?

The Walk

Leaving the pub, turn right up the lane which runs at the side. This goes uphill and in about 200 yards look for a stile in the left hand hedge, just before Larch Cottage. After climbing the stile, turn right into the field and keep inside the hedge to the next stile in the right corner. Still keeping to the right and downhill, make for the gate at the bottom of the field. Turn right into the lane. Pass Pickle Cottage and, ignoring the footpath sign on the left, notice the black and white cottage, dated 1592. It is reputed that this was the site of an ancient monastery. You will probably see that there is a marked difference in the soil beyond the cottage. This is due to the burning of charcoal, which makes the earth very dark.

Just past the cottage is a footpath sign and stile, in the hedge, on the right. Take this and, keeping slightly left, cross the field towards a single tree. Still keeping left, make for the next stile. Marcle Ridge stands out ahead with the radio beacon a very modern addition to the timeless pattern of the fields. Continue straight ahead towards the next gate. Now make for a stile in the very centre of the next hedge and go over the small bridge. Make towards the stream on your right and keep following this until you reach a gate. This leads on to a wide track and past a farmhouse on your right. It can be muddy here at times.

The track now becomes a lane. Continue on this until reaching a footpath sign on the right. Go through the gate and, keeping the hedge on your right, continue straight on. Now walk diagonally across the field towards a stile in the hedge. Turn right into the lane. Continue on this lane, bearing right at the junction and passing some fruit orchards. Just after passing some white railings on your left, take the footpath sign on your right and climb over the stile. Walk diagonally across the field to a bridge over a small stream. Make for the stile in the left corner. Keeping inside the wire fence of this field, make for a stile in the right hand corner. Now make for the gap between the wood on your left and a mound of earth on the right. Continue to follow the path towards a gate in the fence.

Sollers Hope Court now appears ahead, the reputed birthplace of Dick Whittington. Go through the gate or over the stile into the farmyard of the Court. Turn right into the churchyard. The church is of sandstone and is a 14th century restoration of a former Saxon church. It has an interesting early Norman font. Go through the gate into a small field and then over the stream.

Now walk straight on, up the hill, pausing at the top to appreciate the view over the house and church and beyond to the woods and fields of Marcle Ridge. Notice the oast house attached to the buildings of the farm on your left. Make for the left corner of the field and over the stile, an awkward one. Turn to the right round the field, usually planted, and make for the right hand corner where you will need to climb three stiles in quick succession. Now make for the next stile on the right, which will take you into the lane. Turn left and, passing Larch Cottage on your right, continue, downhill, back to the pub.

15 Hoarwithy
The New Harp Inn

+ Carey — "Cottage of Content" v. good food + garden

The New Harp Inn was, originally, two fishermen's cottages. Salmon were netted along the river Wye and this type of cottage was very much in evidence along the banks of the river in and around the village. The Old Mill House stands opposite the pub, with its mill-stones making an attractive background to the flower beds. There was an old pub called the Harp Inn which was situated lower down the road, hence the 'New' in the naming of the present inn. This pub is much used by fishermen and walkers and has a good garden area. Bed and breakfast is also available. Meals are served in the bar, with 'specials' which vary from day to day. Popular choices are beef and beer casserole, steak and kidney pie and some interesting chicken dishes. Home-made soup with crusty roll is another favourite. A children's menu offers a selection of favourite dishes and tea and coffee are served at all times. Beers include Whitbread, Bass on draught and Boddingtons ales. Two local ciders are a popular choice.
  Telephone: 0432 840213.

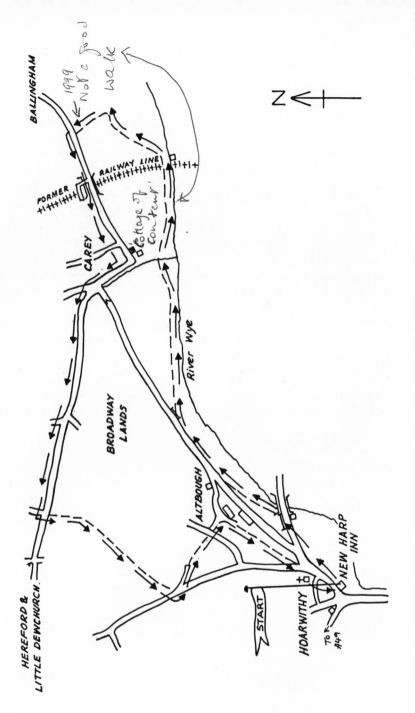

66

How to get there: Hoarwithy is situated to the east of the A49 Hereford–Ross road, 8 miles from Hereford and 6 miles from Ross. The pub is in the middle of the village, turn left after crossing the bridge, if you are coming from the east. If travelling from the A49, you will pass it as you reach the village.

Parking: There is a large car park at the pub.

Length of the walk: 4 miles. Map: OS Landranger 149 Hereford, Leominster and surrounding area (inn GR 546304).

In a beautiful area of Herefordshire this walk takes you a short distance along the banks of the river Wye, with the usual accompaniment of river scenes. Notice the old Toll House, now locked and barred but in excellent condition, still in its place of prominence. The stone pillars of the now dismantled railway straddle the river in independent isolation. These carried the Hereford-Ross-Gloucester line in the days before the useful – but, no doubt, uneconomic – country connections were axed.

There is some lane walking on such minor roads that grass and weeds push their way through the surface. A rather long, steep gradient is experienced after leaving Carey, otherwise meadows and tracks make this a pleasant halfday's walk.

The Walk

From the New Harp, walk through the village and turn right towards the bridge. Take the path, stile and steps down to the river opposite the old Toll House. Follow the river path, crossing a wooden bridge and stile, for approximately ¼ mile. You will see a green footpath sign in the hedge leading to a lane. It is necessary to divert from the river path at this point, due to erosion. Walk along the lane until reaching another footpath sign on the right at a lay-by. Climb the stile here and head back towards the river. Crossing stiles on the way, walk through the watermeadows as far as the pillars of the viaduct.

Turn immediately left after passing under the remains of a bridge and follow the left hand hedge up the field, with the embankment on your left. At the top, turn right, and walk through the first gate on your left onto a lane. Turn left. Almost immediately there is a bridge which crosses the former railway line with, on your right, the attractive conversion of the station master's house adjacent to the station, which was in use, as such, until the late 1960s.

Continue along the lane, ignore the first right turn and pass the Cottage of Content pub. You are now in Carey. Turn right at the next signpost, marked 'Little Dewchurch and Hereford'. Now for the steep bit . . .

At the top of the hill, before reaching a cream-coloured cottage and opposite a turning on the right, turn left into a wide track. Easy walking here with good views across the fields to the river. At the road junction turn left, downhill, passing Stoneways on your right. Just past this house turn right, passing a cottage with a date stone of 1810. Now walk along the track to the road junction.

Turn left towards the village and the pub, but do pause and take a look at the church of St Catherine. Its architecture is unusual, with pillars almost resembling a cloister. Local red sandstone was used to encase the brick walls of the original structure and the white marble altar is inlaid with lapis lazuli, while the central cross is of chrysolite (Tiger Eye).

16 Goodrich
The Cross Keys Inn

The Cross Keys, an old coaching inn, was originally located on the main coach road from Ross to Monmouth. With the coming of the new A40 the pub is now pleasantly adjacent to, but not on, the main road. The bars are large and comfortable with plenty of seating. The lounge, with its open fireplace and beamed ceiling, recalls the days of home cured ham and bacon with the many hooks still hanging from the blackened beams. A ghostly story is attached to the inn and, as a previous publican was a coffin maker, perhaps this is not surprising. Our present-day host offers a warm welcome to customers and a well equipped play area for children with garden seating adds to the facilities. Accommodation is also available.

The bar food is good, home-made and simple. Fresh vegetables and salad platters are a feature and ample, interesting meals are provided for the vegetarian. Those who have a more adventurous palate may welcome a home-made chicken or beef curry or Mexican chilli. The steak and kidney pie in a light pastry makes another good lunch or evening dish. Basket meals, sandwiches and jacket potatoes with a variety of fillings complete the menu. A range of bottled and draught light ales, a choice of lagers and locally brewed Weston's ciders

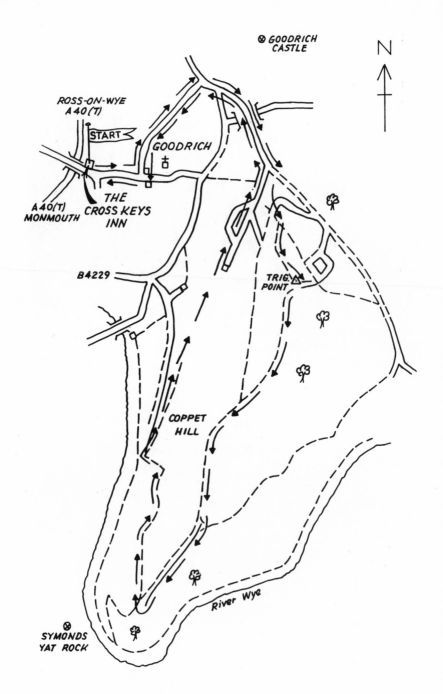

⊗ GOODRICH CASTLE

N ↑

ROSS-ON-WYE
A40(T)

START

GOODRICH

A40(T)
MONMOUTH

THE
CROSS KEYS
INN

B4229

TRIG.
POINT

COPPET
HILL

River Wye

⊗ SYMONDS
YAT ROCK

complement the real ales of Flowers and Boddingtons. For the cider connoisseur, or shall we say addict, there is a brew of 'rough' which will certainly do more than quench the thirst!
Telephone: 0600 890203 or 890650.

How to get there: Follow the signs to Goodrich Castle from the A40 (Ross to Monmouth road). Turn left in the village, by the stores, left again and then right. This will take you to the pub.

Parking: There is plenty of parking space at the pub, but you may like to take your car to the castle car park, which is signposted. A visit to the castle is well worth while.

Length of the walk: 5 miles (or 4½ if starting from the castle car park). Map: OS Landranger 162 Gloucester and Forest of Dean area (inn GR 567188).

A walk to remember . . . a romantic Norman castle, woodlands with a haze of bluebells in the spring, perhaps a glimpse of timid red deer and even peregrine falcons as they fly in the thermals over the river Wye, from their nests in the rocks above. This and more, I promise, as you walk over Coppet Hill Common and take in the views over the Black Mountains.

The Walk

Assuming your car has been parked at the pub, turn on to the lane and keep straight on, downhill, towards the village. Take the first turn left and then the first right. This will bring you to the village stores.

Leave the village by the road marked 'Youth Hostel'. The hill to climb is rather steep but one is well rewarded by the views over the river Wye in about ¼ mile. Turn right at the first fork and then immediately left and follow the sign marked Coppet Hill Common. There is also a footpath sign here. Turn right, up the steps, for a stiff climb through woodland.

The view, on reaching the top, is really beautiful, with the Black Mountains in the far distance and the picture postcard village of Goodrich immediately below.

You will now, after a brief open area, enter some more woodland. Walk down some steps and then uphill again. You should be able to see Symonds Yat, in the distance, clinging to the hillside above the river Wye. Walk on to the trig point.

From here can be seen Goodrich Castle, the Black Mountains straight ahead and the Sugar Loaf Mountain towering over Abergavenny. Behind you are the Malvern Hills.

Continue straight on round a wall, all that remains of a dwelling, into woodland. At a fork, keep straight on. The path is easy to follow but on entering some more woodland it is less defined, although still visible through the trees. Downhill, gently, here and a springtime walk will provide a carpet of bluebells preceded by primroses and daffodils. Wood anemones blow gently in the breeze – this is a really peaceful place.

Once you emerge from the wood, over a stile, the river Wye flows majestically on. Turn right and cross the field towards the river bank. Mallards and swans swim lazily with the current and fishermen try their luck from the banks. Cross over a stile and continue beside the river. It is here, below the woods on the right, that you may be lucky enough to see the deer. Another enchanting sight are the peregrine falcons, flying from their nests in the rocks above the opposite river bank. Buzzards can also be seen joining in the wheeling and circling around the nesting area.

Now keep to the right and make for a gate below the wood. Pass through this and walk along the track. In about 300 yards, a sign 'Coppet Hill Only' can be seen. This is on the right, before the farm and where the public footpath leaves the track and goes into the wood through a gate. Follow the path through the wood, inside the wall. It is interesting to see, here, the locally named 'Pudding Stone', a conglomerate that looks rather like concrete with a mixture of stones in it. It is, however, a relic of the Ice Age, having been washed down, collecting all sorts of debris as it progressed through the valley.

The woodland footpath emerges on to a lane, with violets in the hedgerows in the early spring. Continue along the lane, noting the Old Cider Mill on your left with stones and implements of past use still in evidence in the garden. At the fork, turn left, ignore the footpath sign on the left and continue along the lane until you join the original road you started from. Turn left and retrace your steps either to the castle car park or to the Cross Keys.

Coughton
The Crown Inn

17

This most attractive pub sets the scene for the walk over Howle Hill. It was built in 1857 as a private house, known then as Kiln Cottage when its name obviously reflected the quarries and lime burning kilns, evidence of which can still be seen today. Its charming situation, surrounded by a large car park and garden but in a quiet and secluded part of the village, is a pleasant change from the hustle and bustle of many roadside pubs.

The food offered here is all produced on the premises and I can certainly recommend the tomato and basil soup served with either garlic or fresh bread. Crown cottage pie, bacon, mushroom and pasta bake and cheese and vegetable goulash are mouthwatering dishes. Spicy curried beef with rice, home-baked ham with salad, smoked trout mousse or sweet herrings with bread are also all quite delicious, and the vegetarian meals are tasty and unusual. The selection of sweets includes almond and treacle tart, a delicious meringue and many other delicacies to tempt the most determined dieter. A good Sunday lunch is a speciality. Well kept Whitbread and Flowers Original ales and local

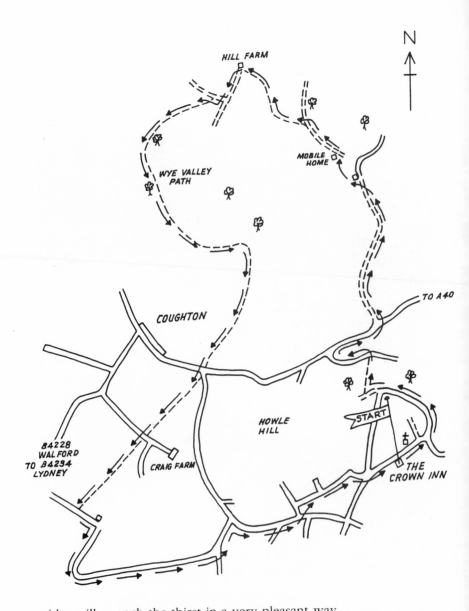

cider will quench the thirst in a very pleasant way.

Opening hours are from 11 am to 2 pm and then from 6.30 pm. Food is not available on Sunday evenings or on Monday lunchtimes.

Telephone: 0989 764316.

How to get there: From Ross-on-Wye, take the B4228 Walford road. On reaching Walford, fork left, signed 'Howle Hill'. Go up a steep hill and turn left at the telephone kiosk, signed ·'Howle Church and Crown Inn'. Turn left into the car park, descending a steep, short slope to do so.

Parking: There is a large car park at the pub.

Length of the walk: 5 miles. Map: OS Landranger 162 Gloucester and Forest of Dean area (inn GR 608207).

This is a delightful walk at any time of the year. It is what may be called 'undulating'. There are two fairly steep climbs but the woodland walking and the wide forestry tracks are very easy and pleasant. In high summer some of the stiles and paths can be partially obscured by the lush undergrowth, but most of the walk is well signed with some of it on the Wye Valley Walk path. The vegetation is varied and at one point, near a deserted house, I found the largest group of purple spotted orchids I have ever seen − a picture indeed. A sheltered walk, and pleasant whatever the weather.

The Walk

Leaving the pub, walk up the hill, passing an old cider press on your left. At the lane, turn left and pass the church. Bear right, then turn left along the track, downhill into a wood. At the fork keep to the right, the path narrows here and can be muddy at times. You now emerge from the woods and can appreciate the views across to the Welsh hills.

Go on to a wide track, a driveway to a house, and at the T junction turn right. Now you are on a forestry track, where the walking is easy and the trees are magnificent. On reaching a lane turn left and, at the next junction, turn right. Continue walking on this lane until reaching a wide, curving bend. Look for the footpath sign, on your left, just round the bend. Now take the gravelled track towards a house and, keeping to the left of the property, continue on the track. Just before reaching a mobile home type dwelling, fork right and go through a narrow gap beside a gate. You are now on a wide woodland track again, a beautiful walkway.

In about 200 yards keep a careful look out for a stile, set back on your left. This is easy to locate in winter but rather overgrown in summer. The path leads up to Hill Farm, which is marked on the OS map.

After climbing the stile, keep to the right hedge, where there is a path. Climb over a gate and turn left into the next field. Keeping to the left for a few yards, climb the stile marked with a yellow arrow. The arrow actually points right − do not go that way, but over the stile into the adjacent field. Turn right, along the wire fence towards

Hill Farm which can now be clearly seen. Still keeping right inside the fence, walk up towards the farm, climb the stile and you will now join the Wye Valley Walk for about ¼ mile.

Turn left, along the wide track, keeping straight on, gently uphill. You will shortly reach a fork where there is a wide grassy track going off to the right. Ignore this, but, leaving the main driveway, just past it, take the path on the right leading into the wood. Follow the arrow, still on the Wye Valley Walk.

Continue through the woods, downhill, quite steeply, following markers. On reaching an open space bear left, down some steps, along a narrowing path. At the bottom of the hill follow the marker along a wide track. When you reach a gate and stile, pass through and walk towards the next marker, which can be seen diagonally right. Keep straight on, left of the post and inside the right hand hedge. Go through the next gate and onto a lane. Turn left.

In about 50 yards there is a footpath sign on the right. Go just up the track and follow the signpost over a stile in the hedge, into the adjacent field. Keep to the left hand hedge towards the wood. Now go over three stiles in quick succession, crossing the road to Craig Farm. Follow the path uphill, bearing left into the next field. Cross the field and go over the next stile (marker sign), to a cottage. Turn right along the track and, at the junction, turn left on a concrete driveway, leaving a white cottage on your left. Continue uphill, winding to the left.

Go straight over at the T junction and then turn left onto a tarmac lane. Pass the Old Post House. At the next junction, The Old Barn, turn left and continue through the village back to the pub.

18 **Much Birch**
The Axe and Cleaver

The Axe and Cleaver owes its name to the heavily wooded area of the ancient forest of Hay. A great need for refreshment would, no doubt, be experienced by the foresters of the 17th century, when the pub was built. An open fireplace lends a comfortable feel to the bar area and the modernisation that has taken place has retained much of the character of this old inn. A spacious beer garden with a play area for children is available for the summer months and children are welcome in the eating areas.

Well kept beers, including Flowers Original, Bass and local ales, along with a good selection of wines are on offer in the neat little bar. A good reputation for food is held and a wide menu is available for both lunchtime and evening meals. Bar snacks include open sandwiches, excellent soups and daily 'blackboard' specials. Vegetarians are well catered for with a choice of pasta dishes as well as the more usual salads and quiches. A separate dining room leads from the bar.

Telephone: 0981 540203.

How to get there: The Axe and Cleaver lies on the A49 Hereford–Ross road about 9 miles south of Hereford.

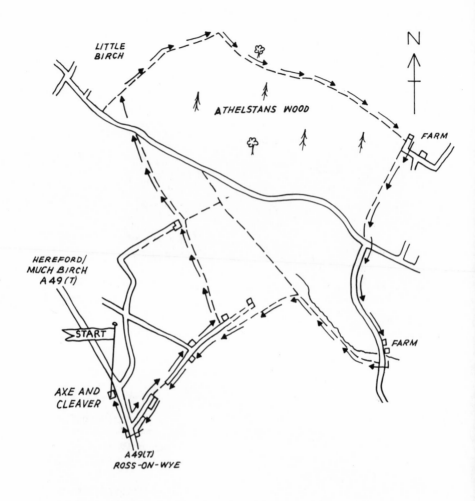

Parking: There is a large car park at the pub.

Length of the walk: 4½ miles. Map: OS Landranger 149 Hereford, Leominster and surrounding area (inn GR 512303).

This route combines a variety of countryside aspects. Woods, fields, flowers, farmyards, animals and birds, it has them all. A family party should enjoy a challenging walk, with some woodland paths in the old Hay Forest and Athelstans Wood, stiles to climb and gates to open. I walked this in the spring when the daffodils in the hedgerows made a wonderful splash of colour.

The Walk

From the Axe and Cleaver, cross the A49 and turn right for a few yards. Turn left into a tarmac lane, passing several houses on your right. The lane soon becomes a bridleway until reaching a metalled road. Note the USA style letterbox outside a cottage here. Continue straight on down the hill, following the private drive and footpath sign. In about 100 yards there is a yellow footpath sign in the left hand hedge. Climb up the slope and cross the stile next to an electricity pylon. Cross the field and make for the stile in the right hand corner. There are then three stiles in quick succession into the neighbouring field. Keep to the left of this field towards the farm. At a metal gate turn right, walking beside some recently planted trees. Make for a large single tree. Climb the next two adjacent stiles and bear left, diagonally, towards an open gateway. After passing through this gap, keep to the right of the next field until reaching a metal gate. Pass through this and turn left along the bridleway. The trees to the right are part of the old Hay Forest and known as Athelstans Wood.

The old bridleway goes uphill and can be muddy in winter. Pass a farm on the right with the sign 'Sydora Herd of Fresians'. Immediately past the farm is a footpath sign on the right, passing through an iron gate. Taking this path, walk alongside the house for a few yards and then go over a stile on the right. You are now in the hamlet of Little Birch.

Climb the stile and turn left, downhill. The ground here falls away rather steeply at the bottom and care is necessary, especially after heavy rain. Keep right when reaching the foot of the hill and walk uphill towards the wood. There is a stile in the corner, giving accesss to it.

There are many fallen trees in this ancient woodland and clearance is a long term task. The bluebells form a beautiful carpet in the spring. Continue up through the clearing and make for a stile straight ahead. After climbing this, follow the hedge to the right, skirting the woodland. You will reach – yet another – stile leading back into the wood. Keep straight ahead here and in about 20 yards you will join the metalled Forestry Commission track. Turn left. The track sweeps round to the right and makes for easy walking downhill. In about 600 yards there is a fork. Ignore both main tracks, cross a small bridge on the left and take a path leading into the woods on the right. After passing a large pond on your right, the path emerges on to a lane. Cross this and walk into the coppice through a gap in the hedge. Continue up through the trees to a gate.

Keep to the right of the wooden posts in the next field, then follow the left hand hedge to the next stile and on to a road. Turn right here, downhill, passing barns on your right and a farm at the bottom of the hill. In about another 300 yards you will see a raised footpath on your right. Take this path, although it may seem that you are walking back on yourself, climb the stile and cross diagonally towards the left hand corner. There are two more stiles here and you are then in a field with a stream on your right.

Walk alongside the stream, cross the water at the footbridge and turn left, keeping alongside the hedge. When the hedge stops and an open field lies ahead, turn right toward some Dutch barns. On reaching a gate, turn left and walk, uphill, towards some farm buildings and silos. The path goes through the farmyard, passing through a gate on your right. Continue into the lane and turn left.

This is the lane used at the beginning of the walk, so retrace your steps on to the bridleway, and so back to the pub.

⑲ Ruckhall
The Ancient Camp

The Ancient Camp may be a strange name for a pub, yet it truly is within an ancient camp – the Iron Age hill fort of Eaton Camp. This 80 ft escarpment commands a breathtaking view along the river Wye. Stone walls and slate floors, many pictures and a sense of history, what more can one want before or after a walk? The inn is over 100 years old and was sympathetically renovated in 1985. It now offers a high standard of comfort both in its lounges and bars and in the accommodation available for a longer stay. Approached down a private drive, away from traffic noise, it has the appearance of a country house. A warm welcome is extended to motorists and walkers alike. Provision is made for sunny days with chairs and tables on the terrace overlooking the river. Children are welcome and there is a special menu for them. The bar menu offers a delicious home-made soup with French bread, smoked Greenland halibut or a ploughman's platter, to quote just a few of the dishes available. A baked ham sandwich with a generous side salad was much enjoyed before I commenced the walk around the hill fort. For a more substantial meal,

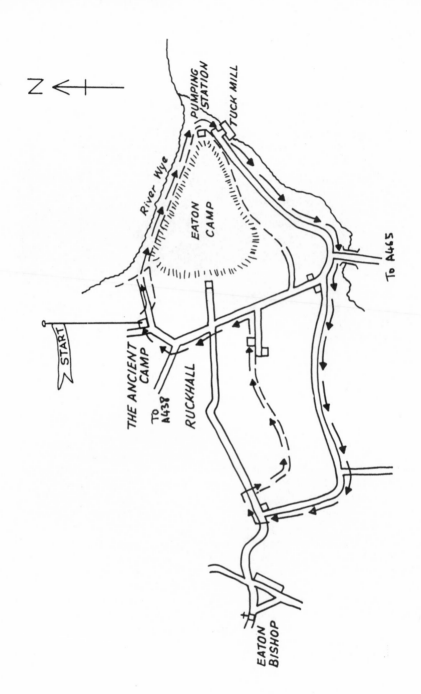

N ←

River Wye

PUMPING STATION

TUCK MILL

EATON CAMP

To A465

START

THE ANCIENT CAMP

To A438

RUCKHALL

EATON BISHOP

perhaps oxtail casserole or poached fresh salmon with new potatoes and crusty bread. Vegetarians can choose from a variety of imaginatively prepared dishes. A separate restaurant caters for full meals and speciality nights are popular throughout the season.

A freehouse, this inn, known to have been a cider house in 1835, now offers a range of well kept beers. Wood Parish Bitter and Whitbread West Country Pale Ale are among the most popular. Lagers and ciders, plus a comprehensive wine list, should be able to cater for most tastes. Opening times are 12 noon to 2.30 pm (closed at Monday lunchtimes) and 6 pm to 11 pm (7 pm to 10.30 pm on Sundays).

Telephone: 0981 250449.

How to get there: From Hereford, take the A465 to Belmont Abbey. Turn right here onto the unclassified road signed 'Ruckall'. Follow signs for the Ancient Camp Inn, which is about 2½ miles from the turn off the main road.

Parking: There is parking at the pub.

Length of the walk: 4 miles (can be shortened to 2½ miles). Map: OS Landranger 149 Hereford, Leominster and surrounding area (inn GR 443391).

The high escarpment of Eaton Camp hill fort overlooks the rolling countryside of the Golden Valley. This is a walk through woods, pleasant quiet lanes and, of course, along the river. You will pass Tuck Mill, which was in existence in 1750, involved in cloth manufacture. You can either return to Ruckhall around the perimeter of the hill, a distance of 2 miles, or walk back to the pub by way of Eaton Bishop.

The area is known for its lush summer growth in the vicinity of the river. I have, therefore, chosen a route that is easily passable at all times of the year.

The Walk

From the pub, take the steps almost opposite the front door down to a path below. Do not go to the bottom of the hill but turn right at the first pathway. The path is rather rough but well trodden. Enter a small wood where the path is wide and easy to follow. On reaching some wooden steps go down towards the river.

Climb the stile and continue along the riverside path until reaching the pumping station. Keep to the right of the building and so on to a wide track. Turn right. You will see Tuck Mill House on your left. Pass through a metal gate and on to a wider track. Do not take the path on the right with the footpath sign, as it can be overgrown in summer. This takes you up to the hill fort. Continue on this wide track and on reaching a junction bear to the right. Notice the well kept lawns and wooden bridge leading to a waterfall on your left. At the next junction turn right. Ignore the next right turn, signed 'Ruckhall', and continue on this lane to the next right turn with two cottages on the corner. (It is here that you can divert and go on into Eaton Bishop to visit the church, but you will have to retrace your steps to here.) Almost immediately there is a sign on the right, beside the cottages, pointing across the field. If planted keep to the left hand hedge and make for the stile in the left hand corner. Go over this and into the adjacent field. Make for a gate near to some buildings. It looks as though you are entering a farmyard. Go through the gate and on to a wide track, passing a house on your left. At the lane, turn left, up the hill and so back to the pub.

20 Orcop
The Fountain Inn

Orcop (the name means 'Top of the Ridge') has always been a village of scattered and isolated farms. There is a group of houses on Orcop Hill but the church stands about a mile away. The site of the motte and bailey castle is nearby and is probably why the church was built here in the late 12th century.

The Fountain Inn is an early 19th century pub, the last of seven inns which flourished in this village. It is a freehouse, with a very friendly atmosphere. There is good, comfortable seating in three rooms. Children are welcome and the large garden area has plenty of tables and chairs so that you can enjoy your pint and meal out of doors, when the weather permits. Bar food includes such home-cooked dishes as soups, salads, basket meals and a choice of sandwiches and curries. I had a delicious home-made vegetable soup with thick crusty bread – a real filler. A local cider from Broom Farm is a popular choice of drink and Bulmers original Fine Mellow is also a firm favourite. Beamish Stout, John Smith's Bitter and Webster's form a collection of good beers.

Telephone: 0981 540304.

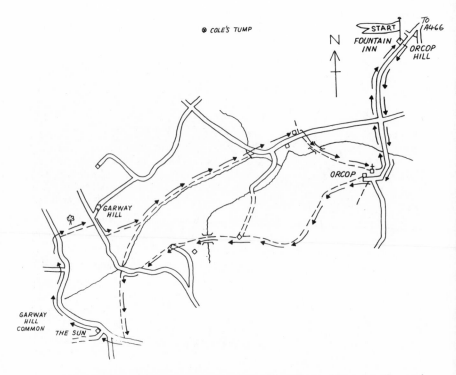

How to get there: Orcop lies west of the Hereford–Monmouth road, the A466. From Hereford take the A49 (Ross road) and branch off onto the A466 for Monmouth. After crossing the B4348 look out for the signpost to Orcop which will be on your right. The pub lies just through the village on the lane leading to the church.

Parking: A large car park is available at the pub. If you wish to walk the shorter distance (5 miles), mainly on paths, it is possible to leave your car close to the church.

Length of the walk: 5 miles or 6½ miles. Map: OS Landranger 161 Abergavenny and the Black Mountains (inn GR 474262).

Winding along field paths and country lanes and on through a wood with an abundance of bluebells in spring, this walk affords a marvellous opportunity for views across to those well-known landmarks of Garway Hill and tree-topped Cole's Tump. There is also a chance to detour to Garway Hill Common. The route is well signed with wide tracks and some steep slopes.

86

The Walk

Leaving the car at the Fountain Inn, walk downhill. An old well near here was the sole source of water for the village until the 1960s. The lane wends its way to a crossroads. Keep straight on, and then slightly uphill until reaching the church.

Walk up the drive to the School House properties, keeping to the left and climbing a stile, signed with a yellow arrow. Turn right, into the field, and continue to the next stile. Go over this and into a ploughed field, keeping to the right. Follow a well defined path which bears left up a steady incline. Pass through a gap and keep to the right of the next gate, with another yellow arrow. Look across to Garway Hill from here.

Make now for the gate slightly to your right and keep to the right of the barn. There is another footpath sign here. Keep right, round the mound of rubber tyres, and continue to the right along the path until reaching another gate. The footpath sign points across the centre of the field, but, should it be cropped, it will probably be more convenient to walk round the edge. You will soon reach another stile. Cross over the bridge (footpath sign). Now make for a lone oak tree and go through the gate on the right. Continue uphill to the next gate, clearly visible, to the right of a barn. Climb the stile. Follow the track uphill. This is a wide bridleway. On reaching the lane turn right. Cole's Tump is now on your right.

Ignore the footpath on your right and walk a few more yards to the one on the left. Climb the stile here, ignore the gate on your left and, keeping to the left of the field, walk inside the hedge. Go over another stile and continue along the left hand hedge. Pass through a gap and, keeping to the right, make for a hedge straight ahead. There is a stile and another footpath sign here. Turn left along the hedge. On reaching a gate walk out on to a lane and turn right.

At the junction keep straight on past a house called The Sun. This was an inn for many years and is now used as a residence. Pass Sun Farm on your right. It is here that a detour can be made onto Garway Hill Common (see signpost).

For the main walk, keep on the lane, passing Dingle Cottage. Ignore the left hand footpath sign and walk straight on. At the next house on the left, take the footpath sign, opposite, climb the stile and keep to the right of the field along the hedge. Go over the next stile and enter the wood, going downhill. Now there are some steps, and bluebells in abundance in spring. Cross the next stile and turn right along a lane. In a few yards there is another footpath sign going through the garden of a newly built house. Cross this into the garden and in a few yards go over a wooden bridge on your right. Follow the track bearing to the left. The path is now easily defined, to the right of the field.

Turn right over a small wooden bridge and continue to keep right, along the side of a small stream. Go over another stile and bridge and then straight on. Keeping to the track and through the next gate, walk diagonally across the next field to a gap. Pass through this and make for another gap ahead. Walk through the next field and diagonally across the adjoining one. There is a stream on the right. Cross the bridge and continue across the field with the goal posts. This brings you into a lane.

Take the next stile on the right, opposite a house called The Laundry. Walk diagonally across this field, over a bridge and into a cultivated field. Turn left. Walk round the hedge until reaching a stile. Cross this field and go over the stile at the back of the house leading into the churchyard. It is now a lane walk back to the car at the Fountain.

21 Abbey Dore
The Neville Arms

The name 'Dore', according to the historian Ekivall, comes from the Welsh word 'dour', meaning 'the stream'. So we have Abbey Dore – the abbey by the stream. The Neville Arms is situated 100 yards from the abbey, above the road and with views over the river Dore to the hills beyond. It was built about a century ago and has been comfortably modernised since. The large bar has a friendly open fire in winter. There is no separate restaurant and food is served in both bar and lounge. Outside there are tables and chairs for the warmer days and children are welcome.

Bar snacks include all the usuals, and an excellent home-made vegetable soup served with thick brown bread, which is very welcome after a morning walk. Sandwiches with a variety of fillings along with ploughman's platters form the basis of this country pub's

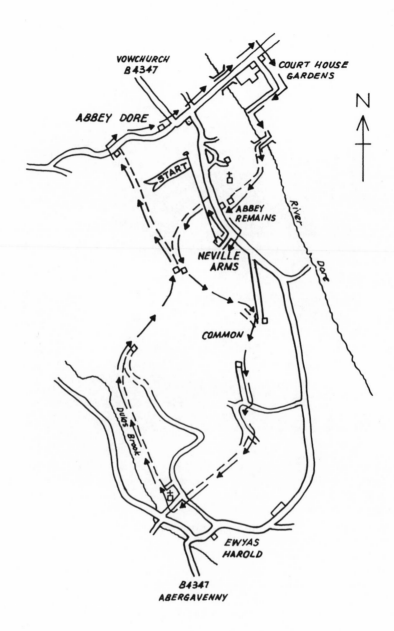

VOWCHURCH
B4347

COURT HOUSE
GARDENS

ABBEY DORE

N

START

River

ABBEY REMAINS

NEVILLE
ARMS

Dore

COMMON

Dulas Brook

EWYAS
HAROLD

B4347
ABERGAVENNY

food. Beers include John Smith's, Bass and Rev James Original, the latter being the favourite among the locals. Lagers on offer are Becks, for those who like a strong drink, and the more usual Heineken and Black Label. There is a good selection of popular, middle of the range wines.

Telephone: 0981 240319.

How to get there: Abbey Dore is on the B4347 (Hay-on-Wye to Monmouth road). The turning off the A465 is either at Pontrilas, passing through Ewyas Harold, or at the English Heritage sign to Abbey Dore. This latter road is unclassified and narrow but easy to follow, passing the abbey before reaching the pub.

Parking: There is parking at the pub and an overflow area beside the road, below the pub, in a layby.

Length of the walk: 3½ miles or 5 miles. Map: OS Landranger 149 Hereford, Leominster and surrounding area (inn GR 385308).

The Golden Valley, a part of Herefordshire which includes this lovely area around the village of Abbey Dore, is very popular with walkers. Its peaceful situation, the presence of the ancient abbey and the views across to the Black Mountains and the Sugar Loaf, overlooking Abergavenny, make this a particularly scenic walk. The river Dore wends its way past the abbey and around the village of Ewyas Harold with commonland stretching above it.

The walk can be 3½ miles, or 5 miles if you want to include the Court House gardens and a delightful stretch of the river.

The Walk

From the Neville Arms, turn left towards the abbey. Opposite the gateway into the abbey there is a stile and footpath sign in the hedge. Climb over this into the field and walk straight ahead, up a steep hill, to the next stile. Go over this and, still continuing straight ahead, make for a single tree at the top of the field. There are good views across to the abbey and MOD ground from here. Turn left, inside the hedge, and make for a gap between a barn and some farm buildings. Bear left between some trees and through the iron gate. Tracks to houses now criss-cross here, but keep straight on. You are now on Ewyas Harold Common.

Continue straight on, crossing various tracks. Where the common closes in there are two forks. Take the left one and walk along a rather muddy track. The common now opens out again with a hill in the near distance, topped with a radio beacon. Keep straight on. As the track separates, keep to the left, passing a studio-type building on your left.

To your right the distant views reach to the Black Mountains, while the strangely shaped Sugar Loaf Mountain, overlooking Abergavenny, looms in the near distance.

On reaching the T junction, with houses to the left, turn right and within a few yards take a left fork. You are now overlooking the village of Ewyas Harold. Go downhill now, for a short distance, over a cattle grid and join a metalled road passing through a small estate of modern houses. Keep straight on until reaching the primary school. Turn right. At the next junction, turn right and go towards the bridge over the Dulas brook.

Do not cross the bridge but take the road immediately before it, turning right into the churchyard. Keeping to the left of the church, pass through an iron gate into a road and immediately opposite into the village playing field. Keep to the left of the pavilion. Pass it and in about 20 yards there is a stile in the hedge on the right. Climb this and keep left alongside the hedge, until reaching a gate on your left. Go through this gate and continue to walk inside the hedge to the double gates ahead. It can be muddy here as the river is very close to the path and is used by farm animals. Look for a stile in the hedge near a single large willow tree. Cross into the field and walk uphill, keeping to the right hand hedge towards the fence at the top. Climb over this fence and onto a track. Turn left. In a few yards is a gate. Go through this and continue, uphill, along the track. This ends at a T junction facing a stone built cottage.

Bear right and uphill towards an iron gate between two cottages. Pass through this and follow the path around the next field. Go through the next gate and turn right towards a derelict wind pump. After passing this relic, turn right, leaving the main track, and walk on a wide, grass-covered path up onto Ewyas Harold Common.

Keep straight ahead for a while and turn left at the next fork. This will bring you back to the studio building and cottages you passed at the beginning of the walk.

You can, at this point, retrace your steps back to the abbey and pub but the full walk continues for a further 1½ miles from here.

Do not turn towards the abbey but walk straight across the field, making for a farm in the far right corner. Go through the farmyard onto the road. Turn right, continue to the next T junction and go straight on. Cross over the bridge and walk towards the Court House gardens, open from the third Saturday in March to the end of October. Immediately past the garden, between the end wall and a house, turn right onto a footpath. This skirts the MOD ground and bears right, making a pleasant walk along the river. Cross the wooden bridge and walk over the field towards the abbey.

Go through the gate into the grounds. The full history of the abbey can be found in a leaflet within the building itself. It is, therefore, sufficient for me to say that from 1147–1536 Cistercian monks inhabited, firstly, a temporary structure here, followed by a later permanent building, still, to this day, the parish church. It is interesting to note that the tower – 'to be built 80 feet to the roof and 24 feet externally, with battlements' – was contracted to David Addams of Ross. He was paid £90 for it, £5 weekly. There is evidence to suggest that this was in or about 1633.

From the abbey grounds, go out to the lane and turn left towards the pub and your car.

22 Bredwardine
The Red Lion Hotel

The Red Lion, a large red-brick building, is situated in the tiny hamlet of Bredwardine, which nestles on the banks of the river Wye. As well as lying below the famous Arthur's Stone, Bredwardine has another claim to fame with *The Kilvert Diaries*. Written by the Reverend Kilvert, who was the incumbent here from 1877 to 1879, these paint a wonderful picture of life in this rural area during the mid Victorian times.

The pub's origins lie in the 17th century, when it was used as a coaching inn. The lounge bears the name 'Courtroom' for it is here that the circuit judge of the day would sit in judgement on the misdeeds of the local population. Today, it is attractively furnished and cosy, with open fires in the winter. A large and well maintained garden with colourful furniture encourages one to eat outdoors on a summer day. There is also comfortable accommodation, with special 'Short Break' programmes all year round.

The reputation of the dining room relies on well prepared, home-cooked food. Prime English beef, spring lamb and fresh vegetables, pheasant and venison from the local estate or fresh Wye salmon from the hotel's own stretch of river are just a few of its justly popular dishes. Bar meals are available with the accent on 'Specials of the Day' on the blackboard menu. Tetley and Ansells Bitter along with Burton Draught are on tap for the beer drinkers, while the cider enthusiasts will enjoy the Scrumpy Jack or Bulmers Original.

Telephone: 0981 500303.

How to get there: Bredwardine lies on the B4352 and is signposted from the A438 (Hereford–Kington road), 12 miles west of Hereford. The pub is at a crossroads in the centre of the village.

Parking: There is ample parking at the pub.

Length of the walk: 5 miles. Map: OS Landranger 148 Presteigne and Hay-on-Wye area (inn GR 332445).

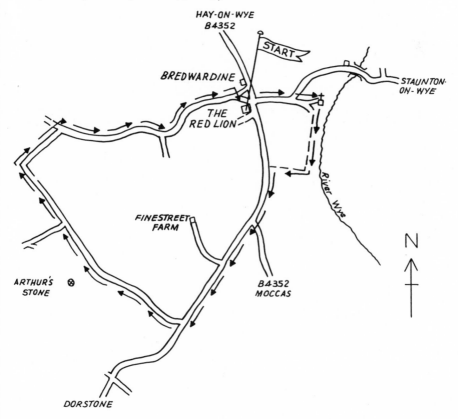

Merbach Hill, part of the range of red sandstone hills which begin in West Wales and reach their summit in the Brecon Beacons, sets the scene for this circuit. A steep climb to begin the walk, flat across the top of the hill, past Arthur's Stone and steeply downhill, back to the car.

A route for all weathers and seasons, sheltered by thick hedgerows that are full of wild roses in the summer and bright holly berries in the winter. It is mainly on unclassified lanes with views across to the Scar, where the Wye has carved its way through the rocks to create a scene of rugged splendour.

The Walk

Leaving the car at the Red Lion, walk eastwards towards the old bridge over the Wye. Just before reaching it, opposite Bridge Cottage, take the track marked 'to the church'. On reaching the church, turn right, along the path in front of the wall, to the iron gate. Go through this and cross the field, bearing to the right. It can be muddy here at times. Go through the wooden gate and then past a pond. At the white post, go over the wooden fence and turn right, following the hedge to the gate onto the B4352.

Turn left here, away from Bredwardine, and very soon turn right towards Dorstone. Continue up the hill, which becomes quite steep. There are views from here down the Wye valley and to the Malvern Hills.

In about 1 mile, turn right, signed 'Arthur's Stone'. Pause awhile at this ancient burial site which, once covered with earth, has now weathered to a commanding antiquity. Its capstone, measuring almost 20 ft, despite having been robbed for road-making material, has survived for nearly 4,000 years. What tales it could tell!

Pass the stone on your left and continue walking on this lane, bearing to the right all the time. Do not go down to Finestreet Farm, which is on the right going down the hill back into Bredwardine. Instead, keep on the lane bending to the left. Continue back into the village where you will arrive with the pub on your right.

23 Hay-on-Wye
The Old Black Lion

Hay-on-Wye is a unique small town on the Welsh border. Known as the 'Town of Books', it houses 14 major bookshops containing well over a million antiquarian and secondhand books and prints, thus making it the largest secondhand bookselling centre in the world. Something of Hay Castle is left, conspicuously posing as a monument to the town's stormy past. Peaceful now, it is encircled by commanding landscapes of the Radnor Forest to the north, the Brecon Beacons to the west and Golden Valley to the east.

In the centre of the town we have the Old Black Lion. Oliver Cromwell was just one of the guests welcomed by this one-time coaching inn which has been accommodating travellers for over 700 years. It is a freehouse, enthusiastically run by the resident proprietors who should be proud of the sympathetic modernisation which enhances the atmosphere of this attractive pub. Accommodation is offered all the year round, with 'bargain breaks' during the winter months.

The restaurant has an international reputation for good food and should satisfy the most discerning, with many English and Welsh speciality dishes included in the menu. The friendly, candlelit bar has

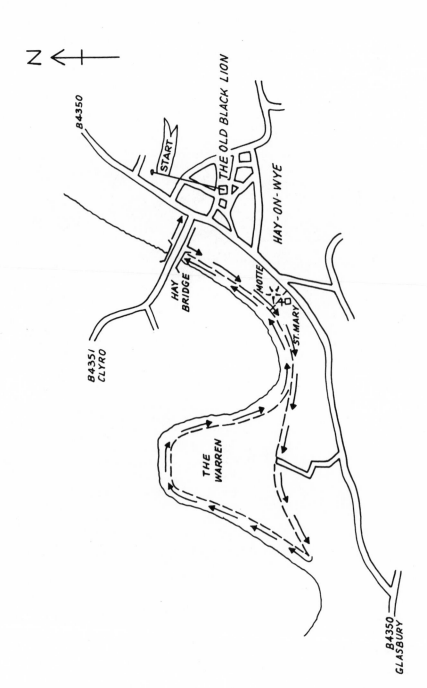

N

B4350

START

THE OLD BLACK LION

HAY-ON-WYE

HAY BRIDGE

MOTTE

ST.MARY

B4351 CLYRO

THE WARREN

B4350 GLASBURY

its own extensive menu with meals to suit all tastes. I sampled smoked trout served with brown bread and butter – quite delicious – while the daily blackboard offered home-made steak and kidney pie, chicken roulade, creamy mushroom crêpes, home-made soup and crusty roll, and well filled sandwiches. Old-fashioned sweets complete the meal, bread and butter pudding being a firm favourite. Vegetarians are catered for with a variety of interesting dishes. Real ales include Flowers Original and a guest beer. House wines by glass or carafe form part of an extensive wine list. Tables and chairs in an attractive garden complete the picture of this comfortable inn overlooking the majestic river Wye.

Telephone: 0497 820841.

How to get there: From the A438 (Hereford–Brecon road), turn off either on the B4351 at Clyro, or on the toll bridge route (B4350). The pub is in Lion Street. Turn left at the market clock and keep left until reaching the pub.

Parking: At the pub or in the public car park opposite the castle.

Length of the walk: 3 miles. Map: OS Landranger 148 Presteigne and Hay-on-Wye area (inn GR 230425).

A first visit to Hay-on-Wye can be a surprise to most people. So many bookshops, a medieval castle with an adjoining mansion, dominating the scene, and the earth motte where once a wooden structure formed an earlier castle. The bailey walk takes us round the defensive wall built to protect the 12th century Norman castle. A town known to have stood many sieges and battles between the English and Welsh, it ceased to be a defensive and administrative centre after 1521. Hay-on-Wye now has a Herefordshire postal address but is administered by the Welsh county of Powys – truly a border town!

An easy walk along the river and out onto the commonland of The Warren, it is suitable for all ages with many points of interest en route.

The Walk

From the pub, turn right and walk downhill, bearing right into the town centre. Make for the clock tower and turn right. Just before the Three Tuns pub turn left towards the river bridge. In front of the bridge, on the right, is a footpath sign. Take this, passing through a picnic area, and go down the steps towards the river. Turn left under the bridge (waymark sign). Continue along the wide track, with the bailey walls on your left and the river on your right. It is here that I saw squirrels frolicking in the bushes.

In about ¼ mile, look for a walker sign on your right. Opposite this is a stone bridge and a flight of steps. Go under the bridge if you would like to make a diversion, on your outward journey, to the parish church of St Mary and see the motte of the Norman castle. Return down the path to rejoin the original walk.

Take the sign for The Warren and pass Warren Cottage. Go through the gate and out onto the common. Choose the upper path here and follow it all round the 19 acres of meadowland. Go through a wicket gate and across a track with two stiles. The footpath now goes to the right along the river bank. Do not continue past the copse. Follow the river round and back to the original gate.

Instead of walking directly back along the track to the bridge where you began, you may well decide to leave the diversion until now and explore the church and motte before making your way back to the pub via the town itself, looking at the many points of interest, including the castle and bookshops, on your way.

Whitney-on-Wye
The Boat Inn

The Boat Inn, well named as it stands almost in the river Wye, has stood here for well over one hundred years – modernised, certainly, but still retaining the character of this riverside location. In days thankfully long past, the otterhunt would begin from here and, no doubt, many a wily salmon has been netted from these banks.

Mine host, resident here for many years, offers a warm welcome to locals and visitors alike. A freehouse, there are well kept real ales with the ever popular John Smith's a firm favourite. Bulmers Original and Strongbow are the ciders served and a good middle of the range wine list is available. The set Sunday lunch is much in demand and an à la carte evening menu is served. Home-made soup with crusty bread was the bar snack I sampled and enjoyed, while the grilled trout looked quite delicious. Home-made faggots and peas may suit some people and the mouthwatering sweets could tempt many. The opening hours are 11 am to 3 pm and 6.30 pm to 11 pm.

Telephone: 0497 831223.

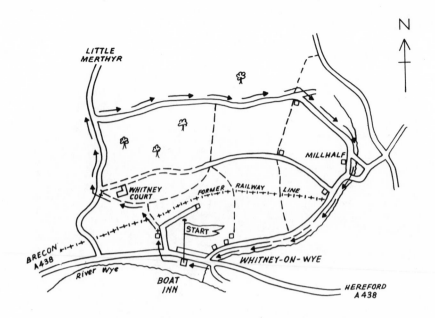

How to get there: Whitney lies 16½ miles from Hereford on the A438 (Hereford–Brecon road). The Boat is on the south side of the main road, by the river.

Parking: There is plenty of parking space at the pub, and limited parking space adjacent to the church.

Length of the walk: 2¾ miles. Map: OS Landranger 148 Presteigne and Hay-on-Wye area (inn GR 268475).

This walk begins at the church, which replaced an earlier one washed away in the great flood of 1735 when the river Wye altered its course. It then goes over the now disused railway line of the Hereford to Hay service, closed in the 1960s, and past Whitney Court, built between 1898 and 1902 for the Hope family.

A gentle walk on lanes which are a picture in the spring with wild flowers. Tree-lined, unclassified and quiet roads make this a walk suitable for all times of the year and for all family groups.

The Walk

From the Boat Inn, walk towards the church, taking care while crossing the busy A road. Walk up the lane on the right of the church and go through the iron gate ahead. Walk uphill through the field towards the wooden bridge ahead. This is where you cross the old railway line. Climb the steps over the bridge and drop down the other side. Turn left, keeping to the path through the woods. You will emerge from the woods into a field where you can now see Whitney Court on your right. With its massive neo-Tudor architecture, this house seems to brood over the valley below.

As the field ends, go through the gate on to a lane, facing a large black and white half-timbered property. Turn right, uphill. This lane now twists and turns as it wends its way through the woods at the back of the Court.

Turn right as you reach the top of the hill and now you have a pleasant walk, gently downhill towards Millhalf. You will pass many beautiful gardens as you make your way towards the village. At the crossroads turn right. There are more signs of the railway line, with a dismantled bridge before you reach Whitney-on-Wye village. Pass through the village and go on to the main road again.

Turn right and you will see the pub ahead, across the road.

25 Kington
The Swan Hotel

Centrally situated in the small market town of Kington, with its half-timbered buildings and quaint shops, the Swan is an ideal place from which to begin this walk. It is warm and comfortable in the winter, spacious and airy in the summer, with a good menu and well kept cellar. A restaurant caters for the more serious diners and the large, comfortably furnished bars for snacks and bar meals. A feature of the pub is its newly acquired 'piste' for the playing of boules, or pétanque to use the proper name. Surrounding this is a pleasant area of chairs and tables for summertime. Children are welcome in all areas and a suitable menu is provided for them. Accommodation is available throughout the year.

The popularity of real ale now takes almost 70 per cent of the beer trade at the Swan. Bass Worthington Best and Hook Norton are most in demand. Keg bitters are well kept and, together with local ciders and a variety of lagers, should cater for most tastes. The restaurant menu offers such delights as peppered steak, flamed in brandy and doused with fresh cream. The vegetarian will be pleased to find a good choice, of which the cheese noodle and nut hot pot is a firm favourite. Among the many tasty snacks are a granary bread, freshly made sandwich with a variety of fillings, or a cheese and bacon toasty served with a generous salad garnish. A delicious home-made soup or, perhaps, a dish of crispy coated vegetables make good starters for a main meal or filling snacks.

Telephone: 0544 230510.

How to get there: Kington lies at the junction of the A44 from Leominster, the A4111, which joins the A438 Hereford – Hay-on-Wye road, and the B4355 Presteigne road. The Swan is situated in the town, close to the information centre.

Parking: The pub has a good car park and there is parking in the square or in Common Close, adjacent to it.

Length of the walk: 4 miles. Map: OS Landranger 148 Presteigne and Hay-on-Wye area (inn GR 305566).

Offa's Dyke, built about AD 780 when Offa was King of Mercia, was never more than 15 ft high, topped with a palisade. More a token bank than a defensive wall between England and Wales, it was used more to restrict the movement of English and Welsh across the border which would often degenerate into skirmish fighting. It is not continuous and in the area between Hereford and Kington only appears in a few places. This route uses a very short length of the dyke but may give you a taste for a more determined effort to 'walk the length' at some future date.

The walk shows you some fine scenery, from the Malverns in Worcestershire to the Black Mountains of Wales, the Brecon Beacons in Powys and the Skirrid in Gwent. There is also a wooded valley, in sharp contrast to the high pasture lands, with its hedgerows of flowers and wildlife, and Kington golf course, the highest in England and Wales.

The Walk

From the Swan, walk into the square, passing then into Common Close. Take the lane leading from the right hand corner of the close and proceed, downhill, over a crossroads, passing through a housing estate. On reaching a stream, known locally as Back Brook, cross this by the wooden footbridge leading on to the town bypass. Carefully cross this main road and take the track directly opposite, signed 'Offa's Dyke Path'. Continue up the track onto Bradnor Green and the golf course. Watch out for flying golf balls.

Follow the Offa's Dyke signposts until, after climbing a stile into a field with a plantation of fir trees, you make for the gate in the left hand corner. The Dyke signpost now points over the hill ahead. Ignore this and turn right, following the hedge to the next stile (yellow arrow waymark). Go over this and on to a lane which leads up to

105

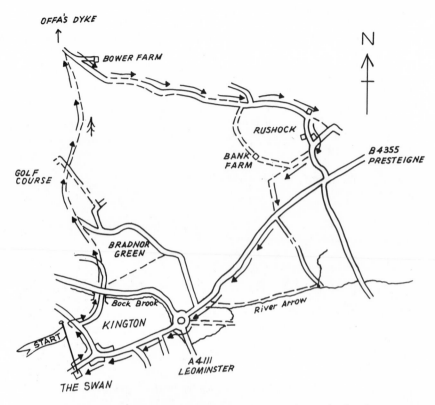

Bower Farm. Turn right, downhill, and pass through the iron gate onto the continuation of the lane down into Rushock hamlet.

Leaving the hamlet, the road bears to the right where you will see a footpath sign on the centre island. Turn right here and follow the track to Bank Farm, marked on the OS map. After crossing the second cattle grid, the track bears right, up to the farm. We go straight on across the field to the next signpost, clearly visible ahead. Follow this, pointing across the field, and make for the right hand corner.

Emerge on to the B4355, Presteigne to Kington road, which is quite busy at times. It is just ½ mile to walk back down into Kington, but, if you prefer to make a longer walk and avoid the road, it is possible to cross straight over, signed 'Mill Farm' and pick up the footpath along the river Arrow and so back into Kington that way.

26 **Pembridge**
The New Inn

Built in 1311, the New Inn is a magnificent example of timber framing. Once a stopover on the London – Aberystwyth coaching route, it was known as 'The Inn without a Name'. In this village of old English grace, with its open market hall, supported by eight oak pillars dated from the early 1500s, time would seem to have stood still. Close to the Welsh border it is not surprising that the troubled times of the 15th century are reflected in the ghostly sightings of a red-coated soldier with a sword. It is believed that the treaty which won the crown of England for the Yorkist leader, Edward IV, was signed in the court room of the New Inn. The village huddles below the church and can boast the same view as in medieval times.

The pub is comfortable, full of character and totally unspoilt. The old furniture and beamed ceilings reflect the passage of time since the day it was built, and a clome oven suggests a totally different concept of cooking. After feasting your eyes on the wealth of artefacts and interesting old books, it is time to feast the 'inner man'. A delicious menu will tempt the appetite, all home-made and with fresh

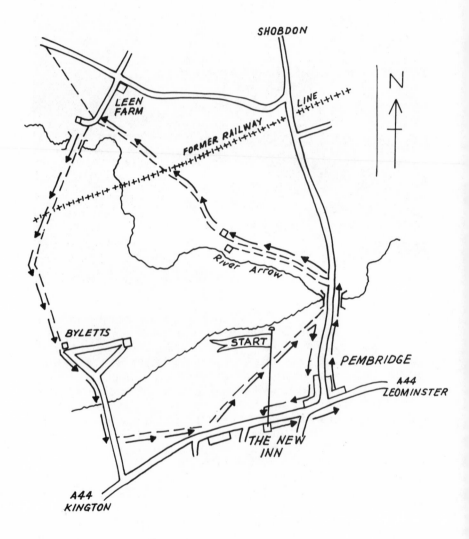

SHOBDON

LEEN
FARM

FORMER RAILWAY LINE

N

River Arrow

BYLETTS

START

PEMBRIDGE

A44
LEOMINSTER

THE NEW
INN

A44
KINGTON

ingredients. Deep-fried Brie with salad and redcurrant jelly, baked avocado and prawns or a chicken lemon casserole are prime examples. Pork steaks, lamb cutlets or game pie are among other tasty dishes. For the lighter moment, a cheese, ham or salad sandwich of crusty French bread, served with a generous salad, is a real meal.

This freehouse serves Ruddles County and Best traditional beer, with Ushers as guest. Beamish Stout and two draught ciders are popular local drinks. A wine list is available and there are good house wines.

Telephone: 054 47 427.

How to get there: Pembridge is on the A44 road, about halfway between Leominster and Kington.

Parking: There is ample parking at the pub, and a public car park adjacent to the bridge over the river Arrow.

Length of the walk: 3½ miles. Map: OS Landranger 149 Hereford, Leominster and surrounding area (inn GR 390582).

This is an exceptionally fine walk for long summer days. Gentle gradients, shady watermeadows and village gardens ablaze with the colour of hanging baskets and flower-filled borders. The paths are well waymarked and the stiles repaired and renewed. There are wide tracks, one being part of the old railway line from Kington to Leominster. Winter walkers should be prepared for muddy patches, particularly after the river has been in flood. Look for the kingfisher and heron along the river bank.

The Walk

Leaving your car in the pub car park, turn right along the A44 for a short distance. Turn left for Shobdon and continue, downhill, over the river Arrow bridge. There are footpath signs, both ways, before crossing the bridge. Ignore these and take the one pointing to the left immediately over the bridge. It is a wide track with a house on the right.

At the next footpath sign, after passing through a gate, bear right around some farm buildings. Go through another gate and cross, diagonally, the next field to a gate in the right hand corner. Now cross over the stile on your left and turn right, keeping inside the right hand hedge towards the waymarked stile in the hedge. Cross the wide green track, part of the Kington–Leominster railway line, and go over the next stone stile, into the field. Keep to the right towards a gate in the right hand corner. This is Leen Farm, marked on the OS map. There is a group of houses here. Turn left in front of Mill Cottage.

Follow the wide track towards a bridge over the river Arrow. Continue on the driveway to the next gate and walk back on to the disused railway line. Turn right. In about 100 yards look for a stile in the left hand hedge, marked with a yellow arrow. Go over this stile into the field. If cropped, keep to the right hand edge and walk round, although the path actually goes through the centre, diagonally. There is a stile and gate in the bottom hedge, waymarked, into a pasture field. Keep to the left here to the house at the top and turn left in front of the house on to a narrow unmade lane.

Byletts House is now visible to the left. Bear right on a tarmac lane. On reaching a footpath sign on the left, go through the metal kissing gate into the field. Cross this field, going towards the opposite hedge, just to the left of the single large oak tree in the middle of the field.

Go through the gate into another field and continue walking until reaching a stile which leads into a housing estate. Continue straight on to the T junction and turn right towards the village and car park.

27 Shobdon
The Bateman Arms

The pub takes its name from the Bateman family, rich landowners whose residence was in Shobdon Court, the pub being the estate home farm and dating from 1650. The lounge, a large comfortable room with an open fireplace, boasts a striking carpet depicting the coat of arms of the family.

The restaurant menu offers the chef's choices of the day, with fish dishes a speciality. Bar snacks are pleasantly varied, with grilled goats' cheese or chargrilled chicken among the favourites. A soup of the day was sampled by the author, this being cream of cauliflower with croûtons and crusty bread – delicious. The vegetarian can expect some interesting dishes. A 'Pudding Club', held on Friday evenings throughout the winter, gives the pudding addict the opportunity to sample a variety of five traditional puddings – dieters beware.

The liquid refreshment includes two traditional ales, Wood Parish Bitter and Boddingtons Keg, a variety of lagers, and Guinness on tap. Opening times are 12 noon to 2.30 pm and 7 pm to 11 pm.

Telephone: 0568 708374.

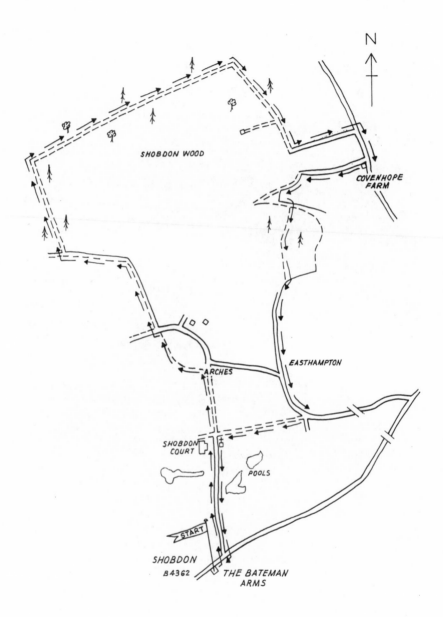

N

SHOBDON WOOD

COVENHOPE
FARM

EASTHAMPTON

ARCHES

SHOBDON
COURT

POOLS

START

SHOBDON
B4362   THE BATEMAN
ARMS

How to get there: Shobdon lies on the B4362, west of Mortimer's Cross (A4110) and north of Pembridge (A44). The pub is almost opposite the entrance to Shobdon Court.

Parking: There is adequate parking at the pub.

Length of the walk: 4½ miles. Map: OS Landranger 148 Presteigne and Hay-on-Wye area (inn GR 402620).

Shobdon Court, a mansion set below the tamed woodlands of the Forestry Commission, is where the walk begins. After passing the Shobdon Arches, you go through woodland of brooding firs and a pleasant open broadleaf coppice. The paths are well defined and easy to walk. You may be lucky enough to spot a herd of deer and you will certainly smell, if not see, both badger and fox. There is a short distance on a permissive path, rather dense in high summer but, at other times of the year, easily defined.

A mansion and church, an archaeological site, woods and fields, flowers and views, this walk has them all.

The Walk

Leave the pub, turn right and cross the road. Enter the gates of Shobdon Court and walk up the drive. The gardens and surrounding parkland are well kept, with vistas sweeping down to the lake with its dainty green metalwork bridge. On reaching the house, continue straight ahead, over a crossroads, onto a long green drive between an avenue of trees. At the top are the archaeologically famous Shobdon Arches. These were removed from the old Norman church once adjacent to the house. Rebuilt in 1850, now decorated in striking blue and white, these arches are all that remain of the previous building. Removed to a place of prominence, dominating the central green lawn driveway, they seem to lure one towards their ancient stones.

Keep left of the arches, along the top of a field, and bear right into a wood on a wide track. At a lane turn left, continue to the footpath sign and turn right. Now turn left into the Forestry Commission area and through a wire gate. Keep left at the fork, passing the Forestry Commission house on your right and a shed on the left. Notice the views here, across to the Black Mountains. Continue on the wide drive and bear right until reaching a crossroads. Go straight across, through dense fir trees and over a log barrier. Pass straight over the next cross-roads, on a narrowing path, until reaching a T junction. Turn right into a lovely mixed wood. An old metal hide is still in situ, rather shaky.

The path now progresses into fir trees again, and it is here that you may see the deer. On reaching a lane, turn left. At the next junction turn right, downhill, and at the farm bear to the right.

In a short distance look on the left for a track with a barrier to prevent wheeled vehicles. Go round the barrier and, in about 300 yards, look carefully, in summer, for a path in the right hedgerow. This is the permissive path, which can be rather overgrown. In about 100 yards the path emerges on to a field, where you keep to the right hand hedge. The path leaves the field through a gap beside a house and joins a lane. Turn left, downhill. Keep left when you join a tarred road and walk down to the first right turn. Take this, leading back into the Shobdon Estate, and so retrace your steps back to the car.

28 Weobley
Ye Olde Salutation Inn

Ye Olde Salutation Inn is a black and white timber-framed building, dating back over 500 years. It is set at the top of Broad Street and commands a good view of the village. A large inglenook fireplace in the comfortable lounge bar is a feature of this old building. The beer garden is a pleasant place to sit in on a warm day. Children are welcome in the eating areas. Accommodation is available at the inn, and one bedroom boasts a luxury four poster bed with a Victorian style bathroom.

The 40 seater Oak Room Restaurant offers a full range of dishes with fresh, local produce, prepared by the owner/chef. However, the rambler may be more than content with the bar menu, which includes such dishes as hot peppered mackerel, smoked bacon and mushroom pancake or a satisfying soup of the day. An even more substantial meal may be had by ordering steak and kidney pie, baked gammon with orange and apricot sauce, prawn and garlic puffs or sweet and sour chicken. Vegetarians are also catered for, with an interesting choice of dishes. The trolley of home-made desserts will easily replace the

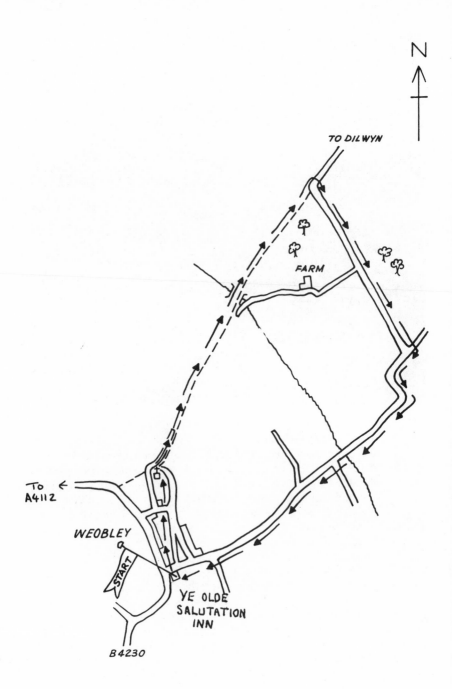

N

TO DILWYN

FARM

TO
A4112

WEOBLEY

START

YE OLDE
SALUTATION
INN

B4230

calories used during the walk described. Hook Norton, Bass and Bonningtons are the real ales served, and a good Welsh bitter, Newquay Steam and Guinness are also available. Stella and Newquay Pils are popular lagers and local ciders include Stowford and Scrumpy Jack. There is a range of malt whiskies and a good wine list.

Telephone: 0544 318443.

How to get there: Weobley lies on the B4230, south of the Leominster–Brecon road, the A4112. It is about 8 miles from Leominster and well signposted.

Parking: There is parking available at the Old Salutation, and a public car park close to the church.

Length of the walk: 4 miles. Map: OS Landranger 149 Hereford, Leominster and surrounding area (inn GR 401523).

The village of Weobley is generally acknowledged to be the finest of the county's medieval villages. Black and white timbered buildings attract the eye from all sides. It lies in the unspoiled countryside of north west Herefordshire and is included in the 'Black and White' trail, along with the nearby village of Dilwyn. The towering spire of the parish church broods over the village and the building we see today was begun in the 13th century. Visitors to the village, in the holiday season, are justifiably many and the paths around the village well used. I have chosen a walk that begins with field paths and returns via a quiet country road. Suitable for all ages, it has no steep hills and the lanes are little used.

The Walk

Leaving the inn, walk through the village towards the church. Keep to the right of the church along a tarmac lane. This narrows in a few yards and, as it reaches a fork, bear right. There is a footpath sign in the hedge here. Walk on for a few yards until reaching a metal gate. Do not go through this but use the stile or go through the gate on the left.

Now in the field, keep to the hedge on the right and continue along this well used path, through a gap into the next field and then through two more gates and past a barn. The church of Dilwyn can be seen from here. Do not take the track up to the farm on the right, but bear left towards a footbridge below and an ash tree. Cross over the bridge and, once through the iron gate, make towards the left side of the woods, across the field. Go through the next gate and keep near to the woods on the right.

When the woods end, make your way towards the gate by the bridleway signpost. Turn right here, on to the lane and slightly uphill towards Home Farm. This is a pleasant lane, bordered by hop fields and orchards. Continue until reaching a junction. Now turn right and walk past more orchards. Wend downhill, back into the village again, passing the Unicorn Hotel and more old timber-framed buildings. You may like to visit a small museum at the end of the walk. This is open from Easter until September and is situated in Back Lane.

Marden
The Volunteer Inn

The Volunteer – how did it get its name? It should be easy to trace, one would think, but despite considerable research I have not yet found the answer, though it is known to have been so called since 1830. For over a century and a half the inn and all the buildings and surrounding land have remained in their entirety. Some sort of record perhaps? Sympathetically modernised during the last few years, the restaurant and lounge area were once the stables. Comfortably furnished with a beamed ceiling they lead out to a garden where one can enjoy a meal and a pint on a sunny day. The bar is a cheerful place where the locals exchange news and visitors are made welcome.

The food is mouthwateringly different: plate-sized Yorkshire puds filled with whatever takes your fancy – well, almost – farmhouse soup, home-made with seasonal produce and served with crusty bread, salmon steaks, fresh fish, fillet and rump steak or, perhaps, a 'Special', a 12–14 oz gammon steak with vegetables or salad. Sunday lunches are a feature with a choice of meats and a Sunday-only price for the house wine. Real ales include Boddingtons Scorpio, a firm favourite among the locals, along with Bass and a 'Cask Collection' of

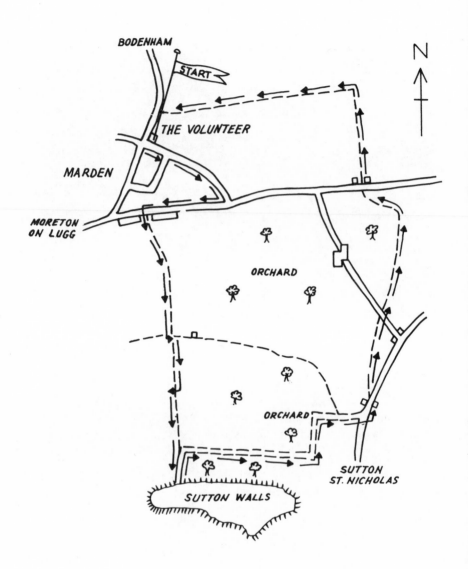

BODENHAM

START

THE VOLUNTEER

MARDEN

MORETON
ON LUGG

ORCHARD

ORCHARD

SUTTON
ST. NICHOLAS

SUTTON WALLS

N

guest beers, as available. The opening hours are 12 noon to 3 pm and 7 pm to 11 pm (Sunday 10.30 pm).

Telephone: 0432 880342.

How to get there: Marden lies east of the A49, Hereford to Leominster road, and can be reached via Moreton on Lugg, about 5 miles from Hereford. In Marden, after passing the lane to the church, take the next left turn and continue to a T junction. The Volunteer is ahead, on your right just round the corner.

Parking: There is plenty of parking space at the pub.

Length of the walk: 3 miles, or 4 miles if walking the fort perimeter. Map: OS Landranger 149 Hereford, Leominster and surrounding area (inn GR 520478).

This undulating walk to the hill fort of Sutton Walls can in no way be deemed strenuous. Apple and pear orchards with their abundance of spring blossom, to be followed by the rich fruit of the autumn, provide a delightful area in which to walk.

We heard a woodpecker as we followed the woodland path and badger sets were evident beneath the trees. A kestrel swooped overhead as we reached the open countryside.

The views across the pastureland of the winding river Lugg, towards the hills and woods of Dinmore, are splendid.

The Walk

From the pub, turn left into the lane which runs alongside. Continue straight on until reaching a T junction. Turn right. In about 100 yards you will see a petrol station and a group of shops. Cross over the road here and walk for a few yards on the pavement in front of some houses, to a footpath sign in the left hand hedge. This could be rather obscured during the summer months. Walk up the path to the right of the sign and climb over a stile. Go through the next gap and, keeping to the left hand hedge, continue straight ahead. In about 100 yards, look for a stile in the left hand hedge and cross over it into the adjacent field. Now, walking slightly uphill, look for a fence in the right hand hedge and cross over this into the field alongside. You have made a slight detour.

Turn left and keep along the hedge, following the well worn path. Go over the next fence, ignoring the stile on your left – you will use this one later – and continue, uphill, towards the wood ahead. Climb the stile into the wood and follow the easily defined path through the trees, bearing to the right.

You are now on the bank of the Sutton Walls hill fort. On reaching the top and the wide cinder track, you may feel like walking the perimeter of the fort (distance about 1 mile). Overgrown in places in the summer, it offers superb views across the low-lying areas surrounding the river Lugg. It is interesting to note that an excavation was commenced here, by Sir Mortimer Wheeler during the 1930s, but not completed and is now infilled.

Now retrace your steps through the wood and back to the stile mentioned, in the right hand hedge as you go down. You will now enter a large acreage of pear and apple tree orchards. Previously owned by the Hereford Co-operative Society, it now belongs to Bulmers. I was there in September and found a small army of pickers busily at work.

The right of way goes through the orchard. Keep to the cinder path, passing various buildings on your right. This main track eventually sweeps to the left. Ignore a left turn and, at the end of the path where it joins a lane, turn left and in a few yards you will see a footpath sign in the left hand hedge. This points slightly diagonally across the field, but you may have to walk round the right hand hedge if the field is cropped. There are two gates in the opposite hedge. Take the second of these and emerge on to a lane. Cross over this and into the field, where a stile is evident just ahead. Follow the footpath and, where there is a division of paths, take the left one. This will bring you to a lane.

Slightly to your right, opposite, there is another footpath sign between two houses. Take this and go over the next stile. Continue straight ahead and through a metal gate. Turn left and make for a row of straggly hawthorn bushes where there is a gap into the next field. Now make for the right hand corner of this pasture, where there is a stile and wooden bridge. Go over this and into the next field. Walk straight ahead, with the cricket pitch on your left, over the next stile, along a path and out on to a lane. Turn left and you are back at the pub.

Hereford
The Castle Pool Hotel

The city was the first Saxon burgh west of the Severn and was granted its first charter by Richard I in 1189. Its lovely cathedral, substantially Norman, houses the 14th century Mappa Mundi and the famous chained library. There are also many museums, ranging from the Regimental Museum to the Bulmer Railway Centre – something for everyone. Hereford, along with most market towns, has a considerable variety of pubs. I have chosen the Castle Pool, centrally situated, close to the start of the walk and with comfortable public rooms and large garden. Barbecues are popular in the summer, with seats and tables close to the water where the drawbridge once spanned the moat to the Castle Green, site of many a memorable jousting tournament. Dating back to 1850, this house was once the residence of the Bishop of Hereford. The conversion to a country style hotel has been carefully carried out.

The restaurant offers a choice of many and varied meals. Perhaps you will choose a starter of smoked cheese and nut salad, followed by grilled Black Mountain trout and a sweet of honeyed apple pie and

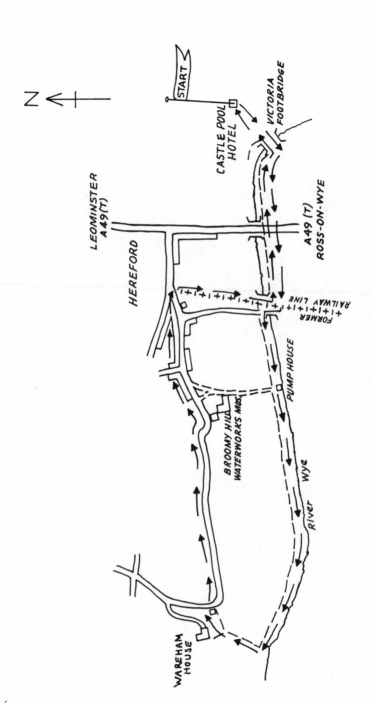

custard, which reflects the local produce. A snack menu, served in the bar, provides one with a tasty choice of dishes, such as soup of the day with crusty bread, jumbo sausage and onions with French fries and French bread, maybe a triple decker sandwich, generously filled with bacon, lettuce and tomato, or a minute steak between two slices of hot buttered toast. A chilli or a curry, fisherman's platter or a vegetarian wholemeal pizza are all attractively served and competitively priced. For the beer drinker, Hook Norton Best, Courage Directors or Wye Valley Brewery HPA are on tap. Wines and lagers and a local cider offer a choice for every taste. A friendly staff and accommodation, should you require it, complete the picture of a town hotel and pub in a country setting.

Telephone: 0432 356321.

How to get there: When approaching Hereford from any direction make for the city centre and take the signs for City Centre East. Follow the road round the pedestrianisation system and keep in the right hand lane to Cantelope Street, on your right. Turn right and then immediately bear right into Castle Street. The hotel is just there, on the left. It is very close to the cathedral but the one-way system prevents approach from that side of the town.

Parking: There is some parking at the hotel and in adjacent streets. However, a public car park can be located by following the road round to the left instead of turning right into Cantelope Street. At the traffic lights, turn left and the car park is about 200 yards on the left. Use the pedestrian exit from the car park, which will bring you out close to Castle Street.

Length of the walk: 3 miles. Map: OS Landranger 149 Hereford, Leominster and surrounding area (inn GR 512399).

Busy little ducks, lazy, elegant swans, brightly coloured canoes and boats, together they create a lively summer scene as you walk along the Wye at Hereford. The wintry wildness of the river creates another scene, just as beautiful, as the water tumbles hastily along its course. Swans and ducks there are, but river people have now housed their crafts until calmer times once more return. The dramatic change in the river level should be noted. It usually manages to flood at least once during the winter months but in the late summer can become very low and almost unnavigable.

There is flat walking along the meandering river path and a gentle gradient to the lane above, with the brooding tower of the Broomy Hill Museum dominating the landscape. The rather grand ironwork of the Victorian railway and footbridge makes a fascinating contrast to the stone of the old Wye Bridge. This circuit offers something of interest every step of the way.

The Walk

From the hotel, walk down Castle Street for a few yards until reaching a turning on the left. This is a footpath to Castle Green. Passing Castle Pool on your left, the only remaining part of the moat which once surrounded Hereford Castle, walk on to the railings above the river. Turn left and then straight ahead towards a flight of wooden steps leading down to the Victoria footbridge. Cross the river and turn right along the path until reaching the Wye Bridge. Built in 1490, damaged in the Civil War and widened in 1826, this bridge still carries a considerable amount of traffic despite the new bridge on the city bypass.

Having crossed the road, rejoin the river path and walk towards the now disused railway bridge ahead. Cross the river by this bridge and turn left along the path, with the cricket ground on your right. The path now wanders beside the river, tarmacked for a while, until reaching open fields. The next mile is on a well defined grass path, passing the river intake station of the Water Board, a white building at the edge of the water.

The magnificent Victorian tower of the Broomy Hill Waterworks Museum looms above. The engines are still steamed at intervals throughout the summer and admission is from the road above. Ducks, swans and other river life are now your companions as you cross a small bridge and climb a stile on your right. This leads up to Wareham House, a 16th century mansion. Pass in front of the house, through a field and onto a tarred lane. Turn right. The view from here is quite surprising, with the Malverns in front and the Woolhope Hills slightly to the right.

Continue walking along the lane, noticing the entrance to the Waterworks Museum on your right and passing some houses, until reaching the path on your right leading to the sports field and the river. Recross the railway bridge and walk back along the path to the Wye Bridge. Retrace your steps to the hotel.